The Concept of the Relevant Product Market

T0326494

Veröffentlichungen des Instituts für deutsches und europäisches Wirtschafts-, Wettbewerbs- und Regulierungsrecht der Freien Universität Berlin

Herausgegeben von Franz Jürgen Säcker

Band 9

PETER LANG

Frankfurt am Main · Berlin · Bern · Bruxelles · New York · Oxford · Wien

Franz Jürgen Säcker

The Concept of the Relevant Product Market

Between Demand-side Substitutability and Supply-side Substitutability in Competition Law

PETER LANG
Internationaler Verlag der Wissenschaften

Bibliographic Information published by the Deutsche Nationalbibliothek
The Deutsche Nationalbibliothek lists this publication in the Deutsche Nationalbibliografie; detailed bibliographic data is available in the internet at <http://www.d-nb.de>.

ISSN 1863-494X
ISBN 978-3-631-57934-3

© Peter Lang GmbH
Internationaler Verlag der Wissenschaften
Frankfurt am Main 2008
All rights reserved.

Printed in Germany 1 2 3 4 5   7

www.peterlang.de

The proper definition of the relevant product market still is the lynchpin of modern competition and merger control law: defining the market too wide makes it impossible to capture the companies' behavioural margins that are the result of market power and are not neutralized by competition; defining the market too narrow creates market power and forces undertakings under the application of Art. 82 EC, Art. 2 ECMR, § 19 German Competition Act and destroys the relative legal certainty that comes with the application of group exemption regulations (cf. e.g. Art. 3 Vertical Agreements Block exemption).

In European and German competition law the aspect of demand-side substitutability has been the most important criterion – it has been taken as absolute and overestimated in its practical effectiveness. The meaning of potential competition and especially of supply-side substitutability as the ultimately decisive criteria has not been systematically grasped.

In economic literature (e.g. *Bishop/Walker*, The Economics of EC Competition Law, 2nd edition 2002; *Kerber/Schwalbe*, Economic Principles of Competition Law, published in: Hirsch/Montag/ Säcker, Competition Law: European Community Practice and Procedure, 2008) clear progress in developing a modern market definition theory can be found. Especially the literature on competitive strategies for implementing or repositioning new products presents methods for defining markets realistically with the help of the companies' marketing plans.

An invitation to speak at the sixth conferences of the Association of European Competition Law Judges (AECLJ) on June 15th 2007 afforded the opportunity to rethink relevant questions of proper market definition.

Franz Jürgen Säcker

January 2008

Contents

Appendices

I

II

III

Table of Abbreviations

AcP	Archiv für die civilistische Praxis
Art.	Article
BB	Betriebs-Berater
BGH	Bundesgerichtshof (German Federal Court of Justice)
BGHZ	Entscheidungen des Bundesgerichtshof in Zivilsachen (German Federal Supreme Court – Report)
BKartA	Federal Cartel Office
Cf.	Compare
CFI	Court of First Instance
COM	Commission
e.g.	For example
EC	European Community; European Community Treaty
ECJ	European Court of Justice
ECLR	European Competition Law Review
ECMR	Council Regulation (EC) No. 139/2004 of 20 January 2004 on the control of concentrations between undertakings (the EC Merger Regulation) (OJ No. L 24/1 of 29 January 2004)
ECR	European Court Report
ECSC	European Coal and Steel Community
ed.	Edited; edition; editor
EEA	European Economic Area
EEC	European Economic Community

etc.	Et cetera
EU	European Union
FIW-Dok.	Dokumentationen des Forschungsinstituts für Wirtschaftsverfassung und Wettbewerb e.V.
Fn.	Footnote
GRUR	Gewerblicher Rechtsschutz und Urheberrecht
GWB	Gesetz gegen Wettbewerbsbeschränkungen of 23 March 2007, BGBl. I, 2007, 2521 (German Competition Act, Law Against Restraints of Trade)
Int.J.Ind.Organ	International Journal of Industrial Organization
Jb.N.St.	Jahrbuch für nationalökonomische Statistik
JuS	Juristische Schulung
KG	Kammergericht (Superior Court of Justice, Berlin)
K&R	Kommunikation & Recht
MünchKommEG-WettbR	
	Münchener Kommentar zum Europäischen und Deutschen Wettbewerbsrecht (Kartellrecht), Band I, Europäisches Wettbewerbsrecht, München 2007
no.	Numero
OJ	Official Journal of the European Communities
OLG	Oberlandesgericht (Higher Regional Court)
p.	Page
Para.	Paragraph
sec.	Section
WettBR	Wettbewerbsrecht

WUW	Wirtschaft und Wettbewerb
WuW	Wirtschaft und Wettbewerb
WuW/E	Wirtschaft und Wettbewerb – Report
WuW/E BGH	Wirtschaft und Wettbewerb – Court Report of the German Federal Supreme Court
WuW/E BKartA	Wirtschaft und Wettbewerb – Report of the Federal Cartel Office
WuW/E DE – R	Wirtschaft und Wettbewerb – Court Report – German Jurisdiction
WuW/E DE – V	Wirtschaft und Wettbewerb – Report – German Administration
WuW/E Eu – R	Wirtschaft und Wettbewerb – Court Report – European Union Jurisdiction
WuW/E OLG	Wirtschaft und Wettbewerb – Decisions of Higher Regional Courts
WuW/E FCO	Wirtschaft und Wettbewerb – Report of the Federal Cartel Office
ZfbF	Zeitschrift für betriebswirtschaftliche Forschung
ZfN	Journal of Economics / Zeitschrift für Nationalökonomie

A. The changing determination of the product market in competition law

I. The function of market determination

The proper economic definition of the relevant product market is – as the European Court of Justice (ECJ) and the Court of First Instance of the European Communities (CFI) have rightly held in their consistent practice – necessary for the appraisal of the consequences of a planned merger on competition.[1] Using the relevant product market as starting point and object of the appraisal can only contribute to a correct assessment of the possible single or collective dominance, if the determination criteria are chosen in a way "to make it possible to assess the actual economic power of the undertaking or undertakings in question".[2] In the second stage of the assessment, whether an undertaking is in a dominant position on a given market, the competition authority enjoys according to settled case law "a broad margin of assessment" since this is "a question of economic appraisal".[3] Mistakes made at the market definition stage, for example through not considering supply-side substitutability and potential competition, will regularly result in non-rectifiable mistakes in the economic assessment of the possibly dominant position. As the CFI has rightly pointed out,[4] in order to avoid narrowing down the market analysis from the beginning "it is necessary first to define the products which, although incapable of being substituted for other products, are sufficiently interchangeable with the undertaking's own products, both as regards their objective charac-

---

[1] See already ECJ, 21. February 1973, 6/72, ECR 1973, 215, para. 32 – Europemballage Corporation und Continental Can Company Inc./ Commission; ECJ, 14. February 1978, 27/76, ECR. 1978, 207, para. 10 – United Brands Company und United Brands Continental BV/Commission; CFI, 30. January 2007, T-340/03 – WuW/E Eu - R 1224, 1225 - France-Télécom/ Commission.

[2] Cf. CFI, 6. June 2002, T 342/99, ECR II-2585, para. 20 – Airtours/Commission.

[3] Cf. CFI, 14. December 2005, T-210/01, para. 489 - GE/Commission.

[4] CFI, 6. June 2002, T 342/99, ECR II-2585, para. 20 – Airtours/Commission.

teristics and the competitive conditions and the structure of supply and demand on the market".[5] The Courts therewith correctly describe the function of market determination as instrument for determining the effectiveness of competitive constraints in a given sector.

The German Federal Court of Justice ("BGH")[6] words this aspect which points to the effectiveness of the competitive process as follows:

„The market determination serves the purpose to determine the competitive constraints, which impact on the concerned undertakings, because for the question, whether an undertaking is in a dominant position, it is crucial, whether the behavioural margin of this undertaking is sufficiently controlled by competition."

To detect this, it is necessary – as the CFI states – to analyse "the structure of supply and demand on the market".[7] From the objec-

---

5   Also ECJ, 14. November 1996, C-333/94 P, ECR 1996, I-5951 para. 10 und 13 – Tetra Pak/Commission; CFI, 6. October 1994, T-83/91, ECR 1994, II-755, para. 63 – Commission/TetraPak.

6   BGH, WuW DE-R 1925, para. 19 - National Geographic II.

7   CFI, 17. December 2003, T-219/99, para. 91 – British Airways/Commission; CFI, 6. June 2002, T 342/99, ECR II-2585, para. 20 – Airtours/Commission; CFI, 28. February 2002, T-86/95, para. 122 - Compagnie générale maritime u.a./Commission; CFI, 21. October 1997, T-229/94, para. 54 – Deutsche Bahn/Commission; CFI, 6. October 1994, T-83/91, ECR 1994, II-755, para. 63 - Tetra Pak/Commission; see also ECJ, 9. November 1983, 322/81, ECR 1983, 3461, para. 37 - Michelin/Commission; CFI, 30. January 2007, T-340/03 – WuW/E Eu – R 1224, 1225 - France-Télécom/ Commission: According to settled case-law, for the purposes of investigating the possibly dominant position of an undertaking on a given product market, the possibilities of competition must be judged in the context of the market comprising the totality of the products or services which, with respect to their characteristics, are particularly suitable for satisfying constant needs and are only to a limited extent interchangeable with other products or services. Moreover, since the determination of the relevant market is useful in assessing whether the undertaking concerned is in a position to prevent effective competition from being maintained and to behave to an appreciable extent independently of its competitors and, in this case, of its service providers, an examination to that end cannot be limited solely to the objective characteristics of the

tives of market determination – as they are defined by case law – it does not follow that demand-side substitution is the sole criterion, but rather that it can be at best one out of several criteria. The German Federal Court of Justice (BGH) has now correctly held in its "National Geographic II" decision of 16. January 2007[8] that "if exclusively the preconceived buying interest of the opposite market side was considered in most cases the relevant market would be extremely small". The classical concept of demand-side substitution, which is used for such market determination, emerges more and more as the Achilles' heel of competition policy.[9] The concept of demand-side substitution is through the exclusive orientation on the preconceived buyer interests associated with the static model of perfect competition and is - without drastic modifications – not able to adequately capture the dynamic developments of most markets.[10] Only with the help of ad-hoc hypotheses, which are based on the criterion of short-term supply-side substitutability, if the demand-side substitutability does not adequately mirror the actual forces on the market, it can be prevented that the relevant market is constructed as an atomized mini-market with a high intensity of competition, which does not need to be controlled. Not alone the existing possibility of demand-side substitution, but also the supply-side substitutability through a short-term switch of production must be taken into account when determining the relevant market, if the purpose of market determination is to be reached.

---

relevant services, but the competitive conditions and the structure of supply and demand on the market must also be taken into consideration.

[8] BGH, WuW DE-R 1925 - National Geographic II.

[9] Cf. Capital, 29. March 2007, 88: „Especially the definition of markets is too rigid and often not modern anymore." (W.D. Ring).

[10] This applies primarily to markets of the so-called „New Economy"; cf. *Ahlborn/Evans/Padilla*, ECLR 2001, 156, 161et seq.; *Pleatsika/Teece*, Int.J.Ind.Organ. 2001, 665ff.; *Padilla*, The Role of Supply-Side Substitution in the Definition of the Relevant Market in Merger Control, A Report for DG Enterprise, European Commission 2001, p. 65ff.

II. The deficits of the concept of demand-side substitutability

1.) Empirical findings

Up to now the concept of demand-side substitution was the established theoretical foundation for the determination of product markets. The ability of undertakings to switch the production without difficulties and in a short term, remained principally out of consideration, even if the undertakings, which under the "pure" aspect of demand-side substitutability belonged to a (narrow) demand market, gazed at dominant undertakings, which had not entered the market yet, like a rabbit caught in a snake's gaze. The EC Commission emphasizes in its Notice on the definition of the Relevant Market (OJ 1997, C-378, n. 13), that „firms are subject to three main sources or competitive constraints: demand substitutability, supply substitutability and potential competition." But at the same time it points out that "demand substitution constitutes the most immediate and effective disciplinary force on the suppliers of a given product, in particular in relation to their pricing decisions." Thus, despite the emphasis of the openness for all criteria potential competition is typically taken into account only for the assessment of the dominant position. The results of the industries and competitors analysing market research, which are processed decision-related by the in-house information and marketing management, remain widely out of consideration, although the therefrom derived competition strategies provide information about how far undertakings, when deciding on the supply of goods and services in respect of price, quantitive and qualitative respect, consider the activities of other undertakings that operate in the same geographic market.[11]

---

[11] For the basic principle cf. *Fritz/von der Oelsnitz*, Marketingstrategien in: Albers/Herrmann (Hrsg.), Handbuch Produktmanagement, 2. ed. 2002, p. 75ff.; *Kotler/Armstrong/Sauders/Wong*, Grundlagen des Marketing, 4. ed. 2007, p. 306ff.; *Porter*, Wettbewerbsstrategien, 10. ed. 1999, p. 86ff.; *Kroebel-Riel/Weinberg*, Konsumentenverhalten, 8. ed. 2003, p. 368ff.; *Trommsdorff*, Konsumentenverhalten, 6. ed. 2004, p. 168ff.; *Kuß*, Marketing-Einführung, 1. ed. 2001, p. 166ff.; *Nieschlag/Dichtl/Hörschgen*, Marke-

Behind each decision related marketing plans stands the question, which is crucial for the market determination: How will the competitive process look like in the future? Which undertakings need to be considered under competitor aspects, if a new product is introduced into the market? How do the undertakings regarded as competitors react, if the price of the product is raised or the quality is changed?

The market determination formula based solely on demand-substitution has proven as less and less sufficient to cover the market determination practice on the national and European level.[12] He, who tries to delineate markets primarily according to the functional interchangeability of products with regard to their characteristics, prices and intended use from the perspective of the opposite market side as the most effective criterion, will in practice be shipwrecked. How unfounded and incorrect the use of the concept of demand-substitution – depending on the functional interchangeability – as main criterion is, show the following examples:

ting, 19. ed. 2002, p. 575ff.; *Homburg/Krohmer*, Marketingmanagement, 2. ed. 2006, p. 561ff.; *Solomon/Bamossy/Askegaard*, Konsumentenverhalten, 2001, p. 246ff.; *Brockhoff*, Produktpolitik, 4. ed. 1999, p. 119ff, 267ff.; *Stahr/Backes*, Markforschung und Informationsmanagement im internationalen Marketing, in: *Hermanns/Wißmeier* (Hrsg.), Internationales Maketing-Management, 1995, p. 69ff.; *Remmerbach*, Markteintrittsentscheidungen, 1988, p. 7ff., 51ff., 114ff.; *Kotler/Bliemel*, Marketing-Management, 9. ed. 1999, p. 391ff.; *Meffert*, Marketing, 8. ed. 1998, p. 174ff.; *ders.*, Marketingforschung und Käuferverhalten, 2. ed. 1992, p. 37ff.; *Herrmann*, Produktmanagement, 1998, p. 135ff., 351ff.; *Koppelmann*, Produktmarketing, 6. ed. 2000, p. 225ff.

[12] Cf. the report of the German Federal Cartel Office (BKartA) (www.bundeskartellamt.de/ Auslegungsgrundsatze.pdf), Cap. VII of the main opinion 1982/1982 („Ökonomische Kriterien für die Rechtsanwendung") of the Monopolies Commission and the Notice 97/C 372/03 of the European Commission on the definition of the fort he purposes of Community competition law (OJ C 372/5); *Engel*, Marktabgrenzung als soziale Konstruktion, 2003, p. 3ff.; *Traugott*, WuW 1998, 929ff.

a)   Markets for ladies- and menswear

The prevailing opinion among scholars assumes one uniform market for ladieswear, menswear, outerwear and inwear. Though, everybody knows that pants are not socks. Even if a market is delineated according to the specific product and one assumes a market for shirts or blouses, a customer who demands a shirt in size 43 has no use for a shirt with a collar size 39. Finally, someone who needs shoes in size 45, cannot do anything with shoes in size 39. For the rational customer shoes in size 45 are not substitutable with shoes in size 39. The same applies to jackets, trousers, socks, etc. The subjective concept of demand-side substitution is misleading.[13] Human beings are not aligned robots, but highly differential creatures.

b)   Markets for air travel

The prevailing opinion among scholars differentiates between "business travel by air" and "leisure travel by air", which is divided again into short-haul and long-haul flights.[14] Someone who has booked a business travel to London cannot do anything with a flight to Paris or Rome, if he has to meet a business partner in London. Someone who has been looking forward for months to his holiday in Greece can normally not do anything with an alternative offer for a travel to Sicily, Spain or Portugal.[15] Someone who wants to make a pilgrimage to the Holy Land will not willingly switch to a travel to Mexico, Salt Lake City or Santiago de Compostela. All these might be – at best – substitution products, but not functionally interchangeable services from the view of the customer, who has

---

[13]   Now also BGH, 16. January 2007, BGH WuW DE-R 1925 - National Geographic II.

[14]   Cf. CFI, 6. June 2002, T-342/99 – Airtours/Commission.

[15]   Someone who wants to go to Attica "his soul still seeking for the land of Greece", does not want to travel to other warm water countries. Who has decided to travel to Rome, does not want to go to Paris or London or vice versa. Nevertheless a uniform market for leisure travel by air to warm countries of middle distance and in European cities, cf. BKartA, WuW/E BKartA 1908, „Lufthansa/f.i.r.s.t.-Reisebüro"; BKartA, WuW/E BKartA 2169, „TUI/Air Conti".

decided to spend his money for a certain intended use. Still, scholars assume a market for air travel to the warm Mediterranean countries, which is supposed to differ from travels to India, Black Africa or Central America.

For the air travellers on short-haul flights it does also not matter, whether the air companies operate big regional jets or jets which are fit for long-haul travel. In contrast, for the suppliers only undertakings with short-haul flights compete against each other, because the operation of typical long-haul jets on short-haul routes is unprofitable. The limited flexibility to switch the offered service leads to a narrowing down of the relevant market even on upstream markets.[16]

c) Market for transport and traffic

From the perspective of the customers containerised maritime transport services are interchangeable with conventional break bulk (line) shipping (e.g. for coffee and fruits). In contrast, from the perspective of the suppliers containerized transports are at best in exceptional circumstances and only in regard to a limited number of products interchangeable with conventional break bulk liner shipping, because the latter is too expensive and break bulk ships can only to a marginal extent be converted to containerised transports. The aspect of supply-side substitution leads here to a narrowing of the market for containerised sea transports, if one wants to be able to describe the existing competitive constraints adequately.[17]

d) Radio broadcasting and television markets

Even in the case of the choice of the desired radio or television programme the market determination does not consider the consumers` wish. The public broadcasting companies do not feel committed

---

16   Cf. CFI, 6. June 2002, T-342/99 – Airtours/Commission.
17   Cf. CFI, 30. September 2003 – Atlantic Container Line and others/Commission T-191/98, T-212/98 and T-214/98.

to the wishes of the average television viewer anyway[18], but see themselves as moral institutions, which are not committed to the Volonté de tout but to the Volonté générale. But at the same time they compete with the private radio broadcasting and television companies. This is why the question arises, whether the assessment of dominance (here: "Meinungsmacht" – i.e. dominant influence of the expression of opinion[19]) must refer to the overall programme of the broadcasting company or to the individual programmes (news, talk shows, entertainment films, quiz shows). From the view of the recipient there is no overall programme, which he chooses; rather he chooses between individual programmes. If he has decided to watch an entertainment film, then he will choose the movie which he finds interesting and is not willing to watch a political, cultural or economic programme instead. Thus from the view of the consumers a functional interchangeability between the different programmes does not exist. Nevertheless the German Commission on Concentration in the Media ("KEK-Commission")[20] does not consider the consumers' wishes in its market determination in its prohibition decision Springer/Sat1. The KEK-Commission defines the markets according to its own views and assesses the dominant position free from any empirical basis.

e)   Markets for books and newspapers

If someone needs a book on family law, in order to satisfy this concrete demand he will not buy a book on competition or criminal law. Nevertheless the German Federal Cartel Office assumes a uniform market for law books.[21]

---

[18]   Cf. *Säcker*, K&R 2006, 49ff.
[19]   Cf. *Eilmansberger*, in: MünchKommEG-WettbR, Art. 82 EC para. 74ff.
[20]   Az.: 293-1 bis -5 (10.1.2006).
[21]   The EC Commission conducts the same market determination, cf. Commission, Case No. IV/M.1377 - Bertelsmann/Wissenschaftsverlag Springer.

The concept of demand-side substitution has also led to misjudgements on the markets for newspapers. The German Federal Cartel Office found that the liberal cosmopolitan weekly paper *Die Zeit* competed with the socialistic *Vorwärts*, the conservative *Rheinische Merkur* and the catholic Sunday paper *Weltbild*.[22] In contrast the Appellate Court[23] found that the *Zeit* competes with the suprareregional daily papers *Frankfurter Allgemeine* and *Süddeutsche Zeitung*. The German Federal High Court[24] found that the *Spiegel* and the *Stern* are magazines that are comparable to the *Zeit*. Three state authorities – three divergent views that were not validated or backed up by public opinion polls. One has to admit that the short time limits for merger control decisions do not leave the administrative authorities the possibility to "escape" into opinion polls.[25] In view of this situation - would it not be wiser to consider the competitive relations, which the undertakings themselves find in their marketing analyses and which are regularly based on market research? These marketing strategic studies are not ad-hoc fictions to reach a certain result in merger control proceedings but strategy papers, which are commissioned to find out whether the combination of the products of the merging parties will lead to synergy effects or whether the products will cannibalise instead of complement each other on the market.

f) Food markets

Someone who only likes dark or mocha chocolate, will – in case of a sellout of both of these chocolate sorts – not regard the offer to buy milk chocolate as interchangeably. Nevertheless the prevailing opinion among scholars assumes a uniform market for chocolate and even includes neighbouring products. Someone who wants to buy alcoholic chocolates will not regard non-alcoholic chocolates as

---

22 BKartA, 9. January 1981, WuW/E BKartA 1863ff.
23 KG Berlin, 24. November 1982, Az.: Kart 11/81.
24 BGHZ 92, 223.
25 See also BGH, WuW DE-R 1925, para. 15 - National Geographic II.

suitable to satisfy the same demand. Someone who wants to buy sauerkraut with sausages as instant meal will not easily switch to ravioli. Nevertheless the courts assume a uniform market for (watery) instant meals and ravioli.[26] Someone who wants to buy orange marmalade because of its bitter taste will not regard strawberry or raspberry jam as interchangeably. Someone who looks for low fat yogurt will not switch to yogurt with a high fat content. Someone who needs cat food will not buy dog food. Nevertheless the relevant market is defined as uniform market for chocolate, marmalade, yogurt, pet food respectively.[27]

g) Beverage markets (Example: tea)

Here the same applies like for the spice markets. All tea sorts are attributed to the same relevant market, although someone who wants to drink black tea to become lively and awake has no use for peppermint, camomile, tranquilizing or laxative teas.

h) Market for presents (Examples: flowers, jewellery)

Someone who is looking in a flower shop for red roses as a present will not be willing to buy tulips, daisies or asters. Nevertheless all cut flowers are put together in one relevant market, because this is appropriate under the aspect of supply-side substitution. Someone who wants to buy a ring in a jewellery store will not buy a necklace or a bracelet. Still a uniform market for gold and silver jewellery is assumed.

i) Markets for technical products

Someone who needs a pointed-top screw has no use for a circular screw. Someone who needs a small screw or a small nut has no use for the respective big screws and nuts. Nevertheless the market is determined as a uniform screw market. Someone who needs a slotted screwdriver cannot do anything with a Phillips head screw-

---

[26] Cf. KG, WuW/E OLG 3759, 3760ff. - Pillbury-Sonnen-Bassermann.
[27] Cf. KG, WuW/E OLG 2403, 2404 – Fertigfutter.

driver. Someone who needs a hammer does not want a chisel. Someone who needs a vacuum cleaner bag for a specific vacuum cleaner has no use for another bag, which only fits into another vacuum cleaner. Only if separate markets emerge from technical specialization (for example in the area of machine tool production), separate markets are determined. Someone who can put at the most a 60 watt light bulb into his lamp has no use for a light bulb of 100 watt.

j)   Market for furniture

Someone who looks for a 60 cm deep closet for his bedroom to put in his wardrobe cannot use a 35 cm deep living room closet. Someone who looks for a table does not want a chair. Nevertheless the opinion prevails that furniture constitutes – differentiated by price class and exclusivity – a uniform market.[28]

2.)   Analysis of the practice

If we ask for the reasons, why scholars and practice have given up the concept of demand-side substitutability in the ten exemplarily shown groups of cases, the answer is easy: To gain competitively acceptable results one tries to avoid atomized mini-markets, which would otherwise be the starting point for merger and abuse control; because in view of the possibility of supply-side substitution of the respective undertakings on a given market these undertakings can easily and within a short time produce "neighbouring products". The willing- and readiness of the undertakings to switch production can be derived from the market studies and the marketing plans that build upon them. The marketing plans include marketing strategies, which consider the existing capacities, the possibility to switch production as well as the profitability of switching production. Not alone the functional interchangeability decides over the

---

[28]   Cf. BKartA, WuW/E DE-V 162, „Porta"; BKartA, 19. November 2001, Az. B9-15/01 – Lutz Österreich/Möbel Engelhardt GmbH&Co.KG; BGH, GRUR 2000, 1108 – Designer-Polstermöbel.

belonging to a market, but also the marketing plan, which takes into account the possibilities of the competitors to enter the market. The formula, that intended use, product characteristics and price, judged from the consumers' view, are the decisive criteria for the market determination has failed in many ways. The intended use of the consumer leads to atomized mini-markets, which make an appropriate judgment on the competitive constraints to which the producers are subject impossible. Every belletristic book, reference book, every shirt, blouse or jacket in a specific size demanded by the consumer is from the intended use of the consumer not substitutable by other products than the specifically demanded products. The decision for a "more economic approach" must apply first and foremost to the determination of the relevant product markets. Legal phrases, which have no instructional value, but barely decorative legitimization function, should be given up. In reality the concept of demand-side substitution is only an intervention criterion for capturing competitive constraints, which impact on an undertaking on the assessed market, but it does not define what needs to be determined. Decisive for the market determination is the short term possibility of the undertakings to switch production and the strength of the potential competition, which both can be found in the market research results of the marketing plans of the undertakings. The concept of demand substitution has lost its theoretical position as most effective main criterion.

Who wants to delineate according to an abstract demand-side market in order to save the demand-side substitutability as "most effective" criterion must ask himself how far he wants to carry the abstraction. Nobody needs "tools" per se. Nobody buys "sweets" or clothing or reference books per se.

Markets which are delineated solely according to the needs of the buyers and their limited willingness to switch to other products are normally much narrower than the relevant product markets which the EC Commission and the German Federal Cartel Office use as the basis for their decisions.[29] These pay – without theoretical backup by the concept of demand-side substitution – more attention to the question of supply-side substitutability[30] and potential competitive constraints, which emanate from undertakings, which are close to the market and capable and willing to enter the market, and broaden the relevant product market through ad hoc hypotheses.[31] The practised market determination is a combination of demand- and supply-side substitutability taking into account the potential competition.

The extent of the existing flexibility to switch production is in Germany and the EC – in contrast to the USA – due to the short merger control time limits usually not determined by public opinion polls or empirical industrial organization studies[32], but by the know-how of the competition authority or the courts[33] in examination of the normally very informed statements of the parties to the proceedings. But the thereby obtained results are not always comprehensible for the outside observer. The "economisation" of the merger control, which finds its significant expression in the new wording of Art. 2 (3) ECMR has not reached the deepened analysis of the market determination and has concentrated on the objectification of the dominance criteria and on substituting the dominance concept by

---

[29] Cf. the references of *Säcker/Füller*, in: Säcker, Berliner Kommentar zum Energierecht 2004, § 19 GWB para. 2ff.; in the older literature cf. the detailed references of *P. Beckmann*, Die Abgrenzung des relevanten Marktes im GWB, 1968, S. 26ff., 109ff.

[30] For the time frame of supply-substitution the Commission assumes a time frame of ca. one year, cf. Fn. 1.

[31] The discussion over the basic concepts of competition law, which had been so intense after the German Competition Act (GWB) entered into force in 1958 (cf. for example *Sandrock*, Grundbegriffe des Gesetzes gegen Wettbewerbsbeschränkungen, 1968), has died down in the last two decades.

[32] Unless such studies are published, cf. for example the market studies used by the CFI in CFI, 14. December 2005, T-210/01 – General Electric/Commission, para. 528, 535, 536.

[33] Cf. BGH, WuW DE-R 1925, para. 15 - National Geographic II.

the concept of significant impediment to effective competition (SIEC).[34] The following considerations try to define the market determination criteria to a larger extent by means of economic criteria and to reflect the practice better in the theory.

From the standpoint of the hitherto existing theory one could now argue: If the theory is appropriate and the practice delineates the markets too broad, one could say – freely adapted from Hegel: "So much the worse for the practice!"[35] In theory everything should remain unaffected as the old is supposedly proved and tested and accurate. But as the preceding examples have shown, it was not the theory that succeeded in determining the relevant markets realistically, but practice, which based its determination on the experience. The theory has produced too narrow determination criteria, which, if applied consistently, would lead to mini-markets. The potential competition and the pace, in which the undertakings can switch production and enter into neighbouring markets with an attractive rentability, have not only an impact on the size of the behavioural margin in the assessment of dominance, but also on the width of the market, on which the competition is set in reality.[36]

Indeed, both the Commission and the Courts stipulate – as initially emphasized – in principle the consideration of supply-side substitutability and potential competition. But with the adherence to demand-side substitutability as the "most effective" criterion[37] it re-

---

[34] Cf. Green Paper on The Review of Council Regulation (EEC) 4064/89, COM (2001) 745/6 final, of 11.12.2001, para. 159ff.; also *Lademann*, Erfahrungswissenschaftliche Ansatzpunkte bei der Marktabgrenzung im Kartellverfahren, 2000, p. 67ff.; *Säcker*, WuW 2003, 1036ff.

[35] Cf. *Wagner*, JuS 1963, 457, 464.

[36] For further reasons why the supply-side substitutability should be considered already at the market definition stage and not only for the purposes of investigating the possibly dominant position of the undertaking cf. *Bishop/Walker*, The Economics of EC Competition, 2. ed. 2002, para. 458; *Motta*, Competition Policy – Theory and Practice, 2004, p. 104f.

[37] CFI, 9. July 2006, T-177/04, para. 99 - Easyjet/Commission.

mains unconsidered that this criterion is in many cases misleading and needs to be corrected, as the German Federal High Court (BGH) has acknowledged now explicitly.[38] The ECJ in contrast sticks to its principle that "the concept of the relevant market in fact implies that there can be effective competition between the products which form part of it and this presupposes that there is a sufficient degree of interchangeability between all the products forming part of the same market in so far as a specific use of such products in concerned."[39] Thus, products which are only to a limited extent interchangeable[40] can – according to the Courts – not belong to the same market.

If the classical criterion of demand-side substitution is used as a basis, an equally balanced inclusion of the criteria of supply-side substitution and potential competition can – at best – confirm and support but not correct the market definition derived from the concept of demand-side substitution. While the marketing and competition strategy in business management[41] has long ago carried out the change from a one-sided consumer perspective to a combined market definition, which also coherently and consistently incorporates the competitors' perspective, this change does not take place in the practice of the competition authorities, as the three criteria, of which

---

[38] BGH, WuW DE-R 1925, National Geographic II.

[39] ECR 1979, 46, para. 28. - Hoffmann-La Roche/Commission; agreeing CFI, 30. September 2003, T-191/98 - Atlantic Container-Line/Commission.

[40] CFI, 30. September 2003, T-191/98, para. 798 - Atlantic Container-Line/ Commission in continuation of ECJ, 9. November 1983, 322/81, ECR 1983, 3461, para. 37 – Michelin/Commission.

[41] Cf. for example *Fritz/von der Oelsnitz*, Markteintrittsstrategien, in: Handbuch Produktmanagement, 2. ed. 2002, p. 77ff.; *Porter*, Wettbewerbsstrategie, 10. ed. 1999, S. 86ff. (System of analysing competitiors); *Kotler/Bliemel* (supra n. 11), 9. ed. 1999, p. 391ff. (analysis of industries and competitors); *Remmerbach*, Markteintrittsentscheidungen, 1988, p. 10ff.; *Stahr/Backes*, Marktforschung und Informationsmanagement im internationalen Marketing, in: *Hermanns/Wißmeier*, Internationales Marketing-Management, 1995, p. 69ff.; *Mühlbacher*, Internationale Produkt- und Programmpolitik, in: Hermanns/Wißmeier, see above, para. 143ff.

the demand-side substitution has an abstract priority, stipulated in the Notice of the Commission, stand unrelated next to each other.

B. History of Dogmas

I. The product market in modern competition theory

The purpose of market determination has been characterized by the founder of modern competition theory, J. M. Clark[42], as follows:

The basic requirement for workable competition is the rivalry between suppliers manifested in presenting the consumer the most attractive offer for "the same product". This rivalry should be the starting point for defining the relevant product market. As far as product markets are concerned, these can be delineated with the help of the following question:

Which products stimulate or discipline an undertaking with regard to the development and sale of its products, thereby restricting its behavioural margin on the market? Or in other words, how far does the competitive pressure derived from the products supplied by other undertakings go?[43] The following questions are significant in determining the existing competitive constraints on the supply-side of a market:

(1)   Which products belong to the *current* supply of the examined undertaking and of undertakings producing products, which are interchangeable according to function, price and intended use?

(2)   Which products belong to the *potential* supply of other undertakings which could act as competitors, either by expanding their distribution area from geographically neighbouring markets (area expansion), or by switching their production to products of the

---

[42]   Toward a Concept of Workable Competition", Proceedings of the American Economic Association, American Economic Review, Bd. 30 (1940), p. 241, 243; for further information *Säcker*, Zielkonflikte und Koordinationsprobleme im deutschen und europäischen Wettbewerbsrecht, 1971, p. 38ff.

[43]   A different question is how *strong* the competitive pressure is. Determining the strength of the competitive pressure is the issue of market dominance or effect of the competitive restriction respectively; here the bilateral structure of the market is taken into account; cf. *Säcker*, BB 1988, p. 416ff.

neighbouring market (product expansion) and then entering that market?

(3)   Which products constrain each other's sale or on which products does the demand concentrate? How does an increase in price of one of these products affect the demand for the other products?

The concept of demand-side substitutability takes into consideration only the products and services, which are covered by the first and the third question. It determines which currently available products the opposite market side deems interchangeable for satisfying a specific demand (flexibility to change demand). In contrast the concept of supply-side substitutability (criterion: which products could be offered by undertakings close to the market short-term to satisfy the consumer's same demand and to increase profits by switching or extending production?) answers the second question. The relevant market is only a "social construction" (Engel) for determining the level playing field, on which in the empirically detectable reality the competitive forces take effect, to which an undertaking feels to be or is exposed. This is why a further step is necessary to answer the question on the definition of the relevant product market: In order to understand the actual competitive process and the undertakings' behaviour not only the objective-morphological structure of the competitive market in terms of the so-called "Marktformenlehre" (doctrine of market forms) is essential, but also the consideration of the undertakings' view as reflected in the marketing strategic studies of the undertakings conducted to determine the marketing and profit potential of the products.[44]

The orientation on the marketing plan of the undertakings is based on the consideration that for competition to function the interactivity between undertakings is essential. This interactivity is not only defined by the current preferences of the buyers, but also by the re-

---

[44]   Cf. *Kerber/Schwalbe*, in: Münchner Kommentar zum Wettbewerbsrecht, Einl. para. 960ff.; also *Remmerbach*, supra n. 11), p. 16ff.

actions of actual and potential competitors. Thus it is insufficient to determine the competitive pressure with the concept of demand-side substitutability taking into account only the opposing market-side's wishes to satisfy the demand ("Bedarfsdeckungswünsche").

The competitive pressure resulting from the competitive forces can only be determined realistically, if one puts oneself in the undertakings' position and examines from their point of view to which competitive constraints their products are subject.[45] The question here is whether a currently significant interactivity with products of other undertakings exists and whether in view of the ability of undertakings close to the market to switch production or from geographically neighbouring markets a market entry of these undertakings is expected.

Thus, the business marketing plans, which consider present and future competitive constraints for the market determination by including the undertakings, which are capable of switching production short-term, is to be preferred to the classical concept of demand-side substitutability.[46] So the pepper market becomes a spice market, the table market a furniture market, the market for air travels to Greece a market for air travels to the warm water countries around the Mediterranean, the costume market a market for ladies wear, the market for short pointed-top screws a market for screws etc.[47]

---

45 Cf. *Clark*, Wettbewerb: Statische Leitbilder und dynamische Aspekte, in: FIW-Dok., Heft 1, S. 47, 51: „In terms of progress this means that the producer determine – and influence- the preferences and significant wishes of their customers and develop the products, which correspond to these wishes."

46 How the undertaking views the relevant product market is reflected in its sales planning and limits at the same time its scope of action, as the undertaking decide on the basis of the prognosed or "felt" competitive pressure.

47 For details see 2c.

II. Demand-side substitutability as decisive criterion in the classical concept of demand-side substitutability

According to the concept of demand-side substitutability the relevant market comprises all products which „according to their characteristics, intended purpose and price are so close to each other that the intelligent (rational) consumer considering them as appropriate to satisfy a specific demand compares them and regards them as mutually interchangeable."[48] Case law[49] and scholars[50] still use this formula as a starting point for market determinations. There is controversy, whether the concept of demand-side substitutability permits the market determination to differentiate markets according to time aspects.[51] Especially the merger control procedures with ref-

---

[48] KG WuW/E OLG 995, 996 „Handpreisauszeichner".

[49] BGH, WuW/E BGH 1435, 1440 Vitamin B-12; BGH, WuW/W BGH 1445, 1447 Valium I; BGH, WuW BGH 1678, 1681 Valium II; BGH, WuW/E BGH 2150, 2153 Edelstahlbestecke; BGH, WuW/E BGH 2575, 2576 Kampffmeyer/Plange; BGH, WuW/E BGH 3026, 3028 Backofenmarkt; BGH, WuW/E BGH 3058, 3062 Pay-TV-Durchleitung; BGH, WuW/E DE-R 357, 358 Feuerwehrgeräte; KG, WuW/E DE-R 35, 36 Großbildfilmprojektoren; KG, WuW/E DE-R 628 Stellenmarkt für Deutschland II; OLG Stuttgart, WuW/E DE-R 48 KfZ-Schilderpräger (Nagold); KG, WuW/E DE-R 94, 96 Hochtief/Philipp Holzmann; OLG München, WuW/E DE-R 251, 252 Fahrzeugdaten. Legislature uses the concept of demand-side substitutability when distinguishing contestable markets from already existing established markets (cf. § 3 Nr. 12b German Telecommunications Act in the version of 24.2.2007: „‚New Market' is a market for services and products, which the rational consumer regards as different from the already existing services and products in performance, operating distance, availability for a larger number of users (mass marketability), price or quality and which do not only substitute the already existing products." German legislature tried with this narrow formula to avoid regulating a market, which it defined as new. This contradicts the EC-market recommendations.

[50] Cf. *Emmerich*, GWB, p. 179; *Möschel*, in: Immenga/Mestmäcker, Kommentar zum Kartellgesetz, 3. ed. 2001, § 19 para. 24; *Harms*, in: Gesetz gegen Wettbewerbsbeschränkungen und Europäisches Kartellrecht, Gemeinschaftskommentar, 4. ed. 1985, § 24 para. 182; *Paschke/Kersten*, in: Frankfurter Kommentar zum Kartellrecht, § 22 para. 63; *Schultz*, in: Langen/Bunte, Kommentar zum deutschen und europäischen Kartellrecht, 9. ed. 2001, Bd. 1, § 19 para. 10.

[51] Dissenting: *Harms*, in: Gesetz gegen Wettbewerbsbeschränkungen und Europäisches Kartellrecht, Gemeinschaftskommentar, § 24 para. 178ff.; affirming: *Ruppelt*, in:

erence to the future have to consider supply-side substitutability and potential competition.[52] Also the Federal Cartel Office uses generally the concept of demand-side substitutability for defining the relevant product markets. Only if the concept of demand-side substitutability generates a market with "no explanatory power"[53] it makes an exemption.[54] In these cases the Federal Cartel Office includes the flexibility of the suppliers to switch production in the market definition: „The relevant product market includes separate product groups, which satisfy a specific demand and for whose development and production a similar research and development and manufacturing know-how as well as comparable manufacturing facilities are necessary."[55]

The ECJ has taken into consideration the criterion of supply-side substitutability in the decision "Continental Can".[56] Although the ECJ considered at first the concept of demand-side substitutability,[57]

Langen/Bunte, Kommentar zum deutschen und europäischen Kartellrecht, § 36 para. 17; *v. Gamm*, in: Festschrift für Gerd Pfeiffer, 1988, p. 648; *Möschel*, in: Immenga/Mestmäcker, Kommentar zum Kartellgesetz, § 19 para. 17.

[52] Affirming: Federal Cartel Office B6-22100-U-104/99 „Beck - Nomos", para. 7; *Hoppmann*, Fusionskontrolle, p. 50; *id.*, Die Abgrenzung des relevanten Marktes im Rahmen der Missbrauchsaufsicht über marktbeherrschende Unternehmen, 1974, p. 37f.; for Art. 82 EC: *Dirksen*, in: Langen/Bunte, Kommentar zum deutschen und europäischen Kartellrecht, Art. 82 EG para. 19; dissenting: Monopolkommission, Hauptgutachten V, para. 611.

[53] WuW/E BKart 2335, 2345 Daimler/MBB. When such a case occurs is not stated.

[54] Cf. BKartA, WuW/E 1840, 1841 „Texaco - Zerssen"; WuW/E 1533, 1535 „Erdgas Schwaben"; AG 1988, 387 „Messer Griesheim - Buse".

[55] Federal Cartel Office (Fn. 51), 2349; also Federal Cartel Office, 8. Februar 2007, B5-1003/06 „Atlas Copc/ABAC", para. 63; cf. also Federal Cartel Office, 14. February 2007, B5-10/07 „Sulzer/Kelmix/Werfo", para. 36, additionally being based on whether the production can be switch short term and without greater additional expenses and risks.

[56] ECR 1973, 215, 248, para. 33 (assessing a merger under the former Art. 86 EC); affirmed by the ECJ in „Michelin", ECR 1983, 3461, 3505.

[57] ECR 1973, 215, 248, para. 32: „...the possibilities of competition can only be judged in relation to those characteristics of the products in question by virtue of

it then asked whether competitors from other areas of the market of light metal packaging would not be able to enter the market by switching production and be strong enough to become serious competitors. In its Notice on the definition of the relevant market[58] the Commission, as mentioned beforehand, emphasized the importance of demand-side substitutability for the market determination.[59] However, supply-side substitutability and potential competition should be taken into account already at the market definition stage, if suppliers are able to switch production in the short term.[60] Even the complete abandonment of the concept of demand-side substitutability can be proper in isolated cases.[61] Through this the concept of demand-side substitutability becomes a combined theory, in which the single elements exist side by side. Hence the Commission divided in the case "McCormick-CPC-Rabobank-Ostmann"[62] the product market into different product groups each characterized by the fact that only a very short time is needed to switch production.[63] The concept of demand-side substitutability was here only of importance insofar as the *general intended* use of the products served as a "starting point" for assessing the ability and time needed to switch production.

which those products are particularly apt to satisfy an inelastic need and are only to a limited extend interchangeable with other products."

[58]   OJ 1997 L 372/5.

[59]   Commission (supra n. 58), para. 13, cf. also the definition of the product market in para. 7: "all those products and/or services which are regarded as interchangeable or substitutable by the consumer, by reason of the products' characteristics, their prices and their intended use."

[60]   Commission (supra n. 58), para. 20, 23.

[61]   Commission (supra n. 58), para. 21. It is astonishing that the Commission refuses to consider the potential competition for the market definition (para. 24) as the extent of the ability to switch production is the most important component of potential competition.

[62]   Commission, 29. October 1993, WuW/E EV, 2157, 2161.

[63]   Though earlier also submarkets, defined with the concept of demand-side substitutability, had been considered as product ranges, cf. Commission, 2.10.1991, WuW/E 1675, 1682, para. 23 „Aerospatiale-Alenia - de Havilland".

The concept of demand-side substitutability tries to capture the competitive pressure, which is exerted on the product of the supplier, only through the degree of the suitability of the product in covering a specific demand judged from the point of view of the consumer. It is correct that the consumers may choose any of the offered products and can play the suppliers off against each other. Only the consumers decide whether the undertaking has the success, for which it fights in the competitive process. This theoretically meets the requirements of optimally protecting the opposing market from market power (at least in the case of short-term consideration). However, in many cases this will lead to small markets, which do not reflect the competitive constraints coming from products close to the market and from potential competition; thus these small markets have to be broadened as the examples under A.II. show. The concept of demand-side substitutability "produces", strictly applied, threats to competition and signals companies "totally out of control", which are not controlled sufficiently by competition. Such a narrow market definition is compatible with the static model of competition. But a modern competition theory, which takes into account innovative, dynamic efficiency aspects of future competition developments as reflected in the market entry strategies of the companies,[64] is not reconcilable with the encapsulation and crustification of markets in terms of the concept of demand-side substitutability, which is oriented to present and past markets and can therefore only consider already existing consumer demands.[65] The need to artificially extend the theory by means of ad hoc-hypotheses unrelated to the theory shows this. Those demanding a "more economic approach" for the determination of competitive advantages

---

[64] Cf. *Thurik/Audretsch*, Review of Industrial Organization 1996, p. 149ff.; *Audretsch/Baumol/Burke*, International Journal of Industrial Organization 2001, p. 613ff.; cf. for the dynamics of the competition process *Schumpeter*, Kapitalismus, Sozialismus und Demokratie, 1942; *Clark*, Competition as a Dynamic Process, 1961.
[65] Cf. *Ahlborn/Evans/Padilla*, ECLR 2001, p. 156, 161ff.; *Pleatsika/Teece*, Int. J. Ind. Org. 2001, p. 655ff.; *Padilla*, ibid. (Fn. 9), p. 65ff.

within Art. 81(3) EC, Art. 82 EC and Art. 2(3) EMCR[66] must consequently also do so for the purpose of a proper market determination that includes market developments.

The preventive, future-related merger control aims call, in order to avoid unneeded prohibitions of concentrations, for taking into account the impact on the market behaviour of the merging undertakings, which derives from other economic subjects, which may enter the market of the merging undertakings within the near future.[67] The market structure or the behaviour of competitors will likely change, if for example competitors exit the market, undertakings produce new rival products or the opposite market-side changes its demand behaviour due to improved information; this must be considered under competition aspects. This is not possible, if one only considers the concept of demand-side substitutability, which takes only into account how supply and demand relate to each other *currently* from the view of the consumer. The behavioural margin the supplier has for future-related decisions on new product developments, investments, marketing activities, marketing structures, prices etc. depends not only on the current demand behaviour. It also depends on the question, which undertakings may enter the market in the future with which new products. Should the undertaking come to the conclusion in its prognosis that a significant price increase will possibly attract new market entrants, it will not

---

[66] *EAGCP* (Economic Advisory Group for Competition Policy), An Economic Approach to Article 82, Report for the DG Competition, 2005; *Monti*, A reformed Competition Policy: Achievements and Challenges for the Future, Speech at the Center for European Reform, 28.10.2004, to be found at http://www.cer.org.uk/pdf/speech_monti_oct04.pdf; *Schmidtchen*, Der „more economic approach" in der Wettbewerbspolitik, German Working Papers in Law and Economics 2005, Article 6, to be found at http://www.bepress.com/cgi/viewcontent.cgi?article=1120 &context= gwp.
[67] Cf. correctly as regards competition theory CFI, ECR 2002 II, p. 2585 Airtours; ECR 2002 II, p. 4071, 4201 Schneider Electric; ECR 2002 II, 4381, 4519 Tetra Laval; cf. *Schohe*, WuW 2003, 359ff.

increase prices in order to avoid additional competitive pressure from newcomers.

III. Extending the consumer perspective by the competition perspective in the concept of supply-side substitutability

The concept of supply-side substitutability assesses the competitive pressure not from the perspective of the consumer, but from the perspective of current and potential competitors. This is because decisions to renew products and to enter markets are made future-oriented. The following example may make this clear. A prohibition decision of the Federal Cartel Office was appealed in a merger control procedure in arguing that no big behavioural margin existed in terms of § 19(1) no. 2 German Competition Act. The undertaking stated that, although having in the long term stable market shares of more than 40% in diverse products, it had to be content with minimum profit margins. High selling prices would have attracted foreign producers due to high profit expectations, which would have entered the German market with mature products. Assuming the argument is correct, the potential competition of the foreign competitors should have been considered by broadening the German market (cp. § 19 (2) no. 2 German Competition Act).[68] Potential competitive pressure, which is considered in the marketing plan of the undertaking, already presently limits the behavioural scope of the undertaking and may therefore not be ignored in a realistic structural analysis of the market situation.[69] The cause of competitive pressure results from the possibility of other undertakings to offer products in a relatively short time which can compete in intended use and price with those of the examined undertaking. Such a market entry can be realistically expected, if companies close to the market share the same "platform technology" or have suitable

---

[68] Cf. BGH, WuW/E BGH 2150, Edelstahlbestecke.
[69] Cf. K. *Markert*, AG 1986, 173ff, who reaches the same conclusion.

"universal facilities"[70] and the necessary product know-how, suitable supply and distribution channels including the necessary financial power.

That it is necessary to include the influence, which potential competitors have on the behaviour of the hypothetical monopolist in the industrial organisation studies, was shown by Baumol/Panzer/ Willig[71] with their theory of contestable markets. Without systematically incorporating potential competition market power cannot be adequately captured. For the broadening of a market it is not enough to expect that the entry of potential competitors into the relevant market is possible. Rather, the specific conditions must be addressed under which potential competition exerts its domesticating influence on neighbouring markets and is therefore considered by the undertakings on the relevant market in their marketing plans.[72] Potential competition affects the relevant market under the following conditions:

a)   potential competitors have spare plant capacity to enter the market within very short time,

b)   market entry does not involve substantial sunk costs (e.g. redeployment and development costs),

---

[70]   U. *Kirschner*, Die Erfassung der Nachfragemacht von Handelsunternehmen, 1988, p. 71; *Kanzenbach/Krüger*, WuW 1990, 472, 478, para. 7 with more references.

[71]   Contestable markets and the Theory of Industry Structure, New York, 1982; *Baumol/Willig*, Sunk Cost, Contestability: Developments since the Book, Oxford Economic Papers 38 (1986) p. 9ff., see for this also *Knieps*, Wettbewerbsökonomie, 2. ed. 2005, p. 28ff.; *v. Weizsäcker*, Kurzgutachten zur Methode der Feststellung von Leitungswettbewerb auf der überregionalen Gas-Fernleitungsebene, 2007, S. 6ff.; *Spence*, Contestable Markets and The Theory of Industry Structure, Journal of Economic Literature 21 (1983), S. 981ff.

[72]   Cf. *Kerber/ Schwalbe*, in: Münchener Kommentar zum Europäischen und Deutschen Wettbewerbsrecht, Bd. I, 2007, para. 1185ff.

c)   no danger of defence strategies, namely limit pricing, of the incumbents, which would jeopardise the attractivity and profitability of the market entry.[73]

Under these three conditions potential competitors must be considered by widening the market definition. Only then it can be prevented that too high market shares on markets, which were defined without considering potential competitive constraints, indicate market power (cf. § 19 (3) German Competition Act) and distort the competition law analysis. Potential competition can force an undertaking, which from the isolated view of the demand-side seems to be a monopolist, to reduce or refrain from prices that are above marginal cost in order to prevent the market entry of potential competitors. Under these circumstances potential competition has the same disciplinary effect as international stock market prices, which take away any pricing leeway from the traders of homogeneous products (e.g. commodities, energy).

The concept of supply-side substitutability on its own does not suffice to determine the relevant product markets. Rather at first the current competitors must be detected by looking at the products, which are already present in the market. These are the products that the average consumer requires to cover his unsatisfied demand, if he should not be able to purchase his primarily preferred product of the undertaking or if this product is too expensive. Insofar the business plan of the undertaking corresponds to the concept of demand-side substitutability. The business plan reflects the consumer behav-

---

[73]   The cellophane fallacy (see for more details *Bishop/Walker* (supra n. 36), p. 122ff.; *Kerber/Schwalbe* (supra n. 44), para. 1164ff. with further references) has made clear that the relevant market can not be defined without a comprehensive competition analysis and that only such products can be included in the relevant market, which are regarded in case of competition analogous prices by the opposing market side as substitutes.

iour with regards to the current competition, and this reflection is investigated by the concept of demand-side substitutability.[74]

An undertaking does not only think of today but also of tomorrow – it assesses the future when it plans investments into products. Nearly every acquisition is an investment in new products, products that are new to the buying company. It will only invest, if an attractive yield corresponds to an adequate risk for the own assets employed.[75] Such a prognosis is only conclusive, if it not only incorporates current, but also potential future competitors in its calculation. The undertaking needs to investigate which foreign undertakings in the future are ready to expand their product range and penetrate the local market from relevant neighbouring markets. Thus, it will adapt its current strategy, quality and price decisions according to the possible behaviour of its future competitors and consider this in its actual marketing strategy. Should the undertaking come to the result that the investment itself does not add up due to the expected market entry of new competitors, it will not invest. On the other hand, should the market analysis come to the result

---

[74] Cf. *Meffert*, Marketingforschung und Käuferverhalten, 2. ed. 1992, p. 47ff..; *Kotler/Bliemel* (supra n. 11), 9. ed. 1999, p. 397ff.

[75] Cf. for the ex-ante determination of the rate of return, which the investor must receive after the company's income tax is subtracted in order for the investment in the relevant market to be profitable: Arbeitskreis „Finanzierung" der Schmalenbach-Gesellschaft Deutsche Gesellschaft für Betriebswirtschaft e.V., Wertorientierte Unternehmenssteuerung mit differenzierten Kapitalkosten, in: ZfbF 1996, p. 543ff.; *Black/Jensen/Scholes*, The capital asset pricing model, in: Jensen, Studies in the Theory of Capital Markets, New York, 1972, p. 79ff.; *Copeland/Westen*, Financial Theory and Corporate Policy, 3. ed. 1992; *Freygang*, Kapitalallokation in diversifizierten Unternehmen, 1993; *Gehrke/Bank*, Finanzierung, 1998; *Gerke*, Risikoadjustierte Bestimmung des Kalkulationszinssatzes in der Stromnetzkalkulation, 2003; *Kruschwitz*, Investitionsrechnung, 6. ed. 1995; *Schmidt/Terberger*, Grundzüge der Investitions- und Finanzierungstheorie, 3. ed. 1996; *Sieben/Maltry*, Netznutzungsentgelte für elektrische Energie, 2003; *Zimmermann*, Schätzung und Prognose von Betawerten, 1997. Should investing according to the undertaking's business plan be profitable, the investment will be made, otherwise the investment will be withdrawn. Insofar the business plan shows how great the competitive pressure is due to the expected market entry.

that a long-term low price strategy will deter other competitors and thus lessen the possibility of significant losses by newcomers, the undertaking will consider this in its marketing concept for the relevant market.

1.) Including the market shares of potential competitors that can switch production within a short time

Potential competitors and undertakings, which can switch to or expand their product range by products that compete for the same consumer demand, should be included in the market determination in order to record the competitive forces realistically – but the question is with which market shares they should be included. Only a market extension solves this problem. As potential competitors can only be such undertakings which already – be it regional or functional – operate in the same field, the turnover of the products close to the market (e.g. all 50 spices[76] or all manuals for legal users) is to be included in the relevant market. By doing so the fact is taken into account that an undertaking needs to develop the ability to enter – with the help of a sufficiently wide product range – the markets of potential competitors with the same know-how and financial power.[77]

Thus, when striving for a competition theory capturing the effective competitive forces, it is necessary to define the relevant market not as a pepper market, but as a spice market and the family law book market as a market for law books. This also applies to the passenger motor vehicle sector, where the car producers have developed from niche suppliers to all-round suppliers producing everything from

---

[76] Federal Cartel Office, 19. July 2002, B2-12/00 – Fuchs Gewürze GmbH&Co.; Commission, 29. October 1993, Case no. IV/M.330 – McCormick/CPC/Rabobank/ Ostmann; Commission, 28. September 2000, Case no. COMP/M.1990 – Unilever/Bestfoods.

[77] The German Federal High Court (BGHZ 71,102 „GKN/Sachs") correctly pointed out this aspect, when it found that a diversified conglomerate, which is close to the market, has a broad product range with regard to technology and marketing.

the smallest passenger car up to the luxury passenger car (VW, DaimlerChrysler, Ford, GM, etc.). One cannot differentiate between smallest, small, lower and upper middle class, superior class and luxury class passenger car markets anymore, but will have to form a uniform passenger car market.[78] Nowadays any of the "big players" is able to produce any car desired by a larger consumer group in a short period of time and to immediately react and adapt to a new model of a competitor. The competitive constraints, under which a passenger car producer presently stands, are not recorded adequately through segmented markets; and also the pressure to adapt and innovate, which derives from an all-encompassing product line, and the nearly infinite supply-side substitutability (from the Smart to the Maybach, from the Lupo up to Bentley) would remain unnoticed.

Especially the example of the market determination for passenger cars, being representative for numerous other product groups and industries, shows that the traditional market determination illustrates a distorted picture of competition. Indeed, the business plan of the passenger car manufacturer shows the worldwide market potential for every single product of the group, which is derived from an enormous amount of detailed empiric data. However, only the whole range of a passenger car manufacturer competes with the whole range of the competitor. The concept of supply-side substitutability serves therefore to extend the narrow concept of demand market to avoid an *"atomisation"* and *"segmentation"* of the markets, which would not illustrate the real competitive constraints. The area of state intervention is thus artificially expanded, although the invisible hand of competition already efficiently limits the behavioural scope of the companies.

§ 19(2) sentence 1 no. 2 German Competition Act implies such an "extended" market determination: The "paramount market posi-

---

[78] Different Federal Cartel Office, Tätigkeitsbericht 1961, p. 23; 1964, p. 24.

tion" ("überlegene Marktstellung") refers to the control of the paramount behavioural margin, no matter where it derives from. To define the market has only one purpose: to analogously determine the area, in which a company is subject to a significant competitive pressure of other undertakings and through this forfeits its dominant market position. The market definition as well as the subsequent appraisal of market dominance is only a means to an end – they aim to answer the question whether for instance a merger creates or strengthens a behavioural margin not controlled by competition. A narrow market determination would fictively diminish the number of competitors; then – in view of the high market shares – a relatively low competitive pressure would suffice to find a dominant position. The competition of substitution goods, affecting all market participants equally, would be blanked out contrary to competitive reality.[79] In contrast a too wide market definition would result in significantly smaller market shares. A superior behavioural margin can then only be derived from grounds not connected to market shares (cf. for instance the criteria in § 19(2) sentence 1 no. 2 German Competition Act).

The concept of demand-side substitution leads for instance to a market for "textbooks on European Law" as a relevant product market. In contrast, the concept of supply-side substitutability would create a market for law textbooks for professional legal users, since the necessary know-how is able to be used to create textbooks for all legal areas. Thus all suppliers of law textbooks are competitors in that relevant market.[80]

In contrast to the pure concept of demand-side substitutability, the concept of supply-side substitutability provides for a balance be-

---

[79] BGH, WuW/E BGH 2112, Gruner & Jahr – Zeit I; BGH, WuW/E BGH 3026 Backofenmarkt; Säcker/Füller (supra n. 29), para. 66 with further references.
[80] Cf. Federal Cartel Office B6-22100-U-104/99 „Beck - Nomos"; see also Golz, Der sachlich relevante Markt bei Verlagserzeugnissen, p. 206 (demand market), p. 227 (supply-side substitutability), p. 258f. (business plan).

tween *short term and long term competition and consumer protection.*[81] Similarly it prevents the creation of isolated "islands", into which dominant undertakings can enter neither through acquisition (Art. 2 EMCR) nor through a squeezing out with price strategies in terms of Art. 82 EC, § 20(4) German Competition Act. This results in a slowing down of competition, as the undertakings on this market are not threatened by big companies entering to market.

The Commission only seldom applies the concept of supply-side substitutability when defining the market. There are no clear criteria in which cases the Commission broadens the market. The Commission does not sufficiently consider the dynamic development of the market. The Commission makes the consideration of supply-side substitutability dependent on whether it is present at the time of the appraisal; as the decisive criterion the Commission uses the technological feasibility of switching production.[82] According to the Commission markets will only be aggregated in response to supply-side constraints when supply-side substitutability is nearly universal, i.e. production substitution among a group of products is found to be technologically feasible and economically viable for most, if not all, firms selling one or more of those products.[83] In DuPont/ICI the

---

[81] „McCormick - CPC - Rabobank - Ostmann" (Commission, 29.10.1993, WuW/E EV 2157, 2161); „Karstadt - Lufthansa" or „Preussag - Hapag-Loyd - TUI" (BKartA WuW 1998, 566ff.).

[82] Cf. for the Commission's practice *Padilla*, The Role of Supply-side Substitution in the Definition of the Relevant Market in Merger Control, A Report for DG Enterprise, European Commission 2001, to be found at http://ec.europa.eu/enterprise/library/lib-competition/doc/supply-side_substitution.pdf.

[83] *Padilla*, The Role of Supply-side Substitution in the Definition of the Relevant Market in Merger Control, A Report for DG Enterprise, European Commission 2001, to be found at http://ec.europa.eu/enterprise/library/lib-competition/doc/supply-side_substitution.pdf, p. 23. So the Commission seem to use the criterion of "near universal substitutability", which the US Horizontal Merger Guidelines explicitly require for the consideration of supply-side substitutability (Department of Justice and Federal Trade Commission, Horizontal Merger Guidelines 1992, sec. 1.321 para. 14).

market was aggregated on the grounds that all suppliers offered or could offer the full range of Titanium Dioxide grades.[84] In Agfa-Gevaert/DuPont the Commission did not take into consideration supply-side substitution (switching from positive to negative plates) as "only some producers actually manufacture[d] all types of plates".[85] But if no account is taken of the competitive constraints exerted by "some" companies – only because supply-side substitution is not nearly universal –, the market shares of the undertaking in question would be necessarily overestimated.[86] The Commission concentrates in its analysis on the technological feasibility of switching production at the time of the notification of the merger. But the decisive criterion should rather be whether the producers have the economic incentives to switch production with immediacy.[87]

In the following section it will be shown that this weakness of the current practice could be solved, if the criterion of supply-side substitutability was included in the market definition under the concept of business plans.

2.) Including the competitive constraints by taking into account the marketing plans of the undertakings

In order to register which economic subjects are in competition with each other in a future-related forecast, only the concept considering the business plans of the undertakings, which combines supply- and demand-side substitutability, will present the most precise

---

[84] Commission, 02. October 1997, Case no. IV/M.984, para. 41 - DuPont/ICI.

[85] Commission, 11. February 1998, Case no. IV/M.986 para. 26 - Agfa-Gevaert/Du Pont.

[86] Cf. consenting *Padilla* (supra n. 10), p. 36.

[87] In the case DuPont/ICI the Commission defined a single market for all grades of titanium dioxide, because to switch production from one grade to another was technologically feasible. This was found although the producers wanting to switch had to commit their capacities via long-term contracts to customers; Commission, 02. Oktober 1997, Case no. IV/M.984, para. 38 and 41 - DuPont/ICI; *Padilla* (supra n. 10), p. 45.

forecast:[88] The decisive criterion is which already marketed or soon-to-be-introduced products of other undertakings a vendor of a product takes into account when changing the price or the quality of his products.

The marketing and competitive strategies of the undertakings are not solely defined through the objective structure of the relevant market, as assumed by the classical, market-morphological[89] price theory. Modern price theory rather assumes pricing and competition to be influenced by market strategic behaviour, competition consciousness of the undertakings and the competitive strategy resulting from these factors.[90] However, realising this should not mislead about the fact that the objective market structure is the determining basis for drawing up the subjective business plan. A polypolist behaving like a monopolist due to a wrong appraisal of the objective market structure would very quickly come upon its limits and notice its wrong market appraisal.[91]

---

[88] Cf. *Mestmäcker*, Das marktbeherrschende Unternehmen im Recht der Wettbewerbsbeschränkungen, 1959, p. 9ff. and *W. Eucken*, Grundlagen der Nationalökonomie, 6. ed. 1959, p. 93ff., who only refer to the business plan of the undertaking.

[89] *J. Robinson*, The Economics of Imperfect Competition, 1933; *Chamberlain*, The Theory of Monopolistic Competition, 1933; *Triffin*, Monopolistic Competition and General Equilibrium Theory, 1940; in the German lieteratur cf. *v. Stackelberg*, Marktform und Gleichgewicht, 1934; *Sandrock*, Grundbegriffe des GWB, 1968, p. 85ff.

[90] *R. Frisch*, La Notion de Force dans l'Economie, in: Festschrift für Westergaard, National okonomisk Tidsskrift 71 (1933), p. 252ff.; *E. Schneider*, Jb.N.St. 157 (1943), p. 406ff.; *Ott*, Marktreform und Verhaltensweise, 1959, p. 18ff., *Heuß*, Allgemeine Markttheorie, 1965, p. 265ff.; *Hoppmann*, Jb.N.St. 1979 (1966), p. 286, 305ff. und 184 (1970), p. 397, 409; *Krüsselberg*, Marktwirtschaft und ökonomische Theorie, 1969, p. 34ff.; *Herdzina*, Einführung in die Mikroökonomik, 2. ed. 1991, p. 110; from an management point of view *Kotler/Bliemel* (supra n. 11), p. 403ff.

[91] The market form is neither an objectively predetermined form nor an identification of possible competition forms, which is only possible from an ex post view. A theory can only be practicable in competition policy, if it considers the conjectural marketing strategy of the undertaking that includes the consideration of the market structure; cf. Willeke, HDSW 7 (1961), 136, 144; cf. *Shubik*, ZfN XVII (1957), 191ff.; *Ma-*

46

The concept of business plans and its systematic connection of sup-
ply- and demand-side substitutability is closer to the competitive
reality than all the other one-dimensional market determination
theories: The market structure is competition-intensive, if the winning margin, which an undertaking receives through technical progress, is "eaten up"[92] by competitors within short time and consumers resort to rival products, if price increases or deteriorations in
quality occur. If a lively product competition exists according to the
assessment of an undertaking, than it will take into consideration in
his competitive strategy the interdependence between its products
and current and potential rival products as well as the products,
which can be introduced by undertakings through switching production short term. Should the undertaking feel no significant competition, it will make its decisions on price, output level and product quality without considering the competitors. The business plan
mirrors the objective market structure reflected by the undertaking.

The pricing in heterogeneous competition, however, is not objectively determined by morphological data. Rather, there exist market
strategic behavioural margins,[93] which leave it to the undertaking to
decide whether to react to new competing offers by a decrease in
price, an increase in quality or by advertising campaigns with the
aim to form stronger subjective product preferences with the customer. A reality-related competition theory will always have to as-
sert the market structure and the market behaviour as the reaction
to the market structure. Economic behaviour – may it be unilateral
measures, cooperation or mergers – is shaped not only through the
existing market form, but it is also constructed to change this mar-

---

son, Harvard Economic Studies 100 (1957), 34ff.; *Krelle*, Preistheorie, 1961, p. 41ff.;
Niehaus, Schw. ZVSt. 90 (1954), 145ff.; *Machlup*, Wettbewerb im Verkauf, 1966, p. 77ff.
[92] *Niehaus*, in: Schweizerische Zeitschrift für Volkswirtschaft und Statistik, 90. Jahr-
gang (1954), 145, 156.
[93] *Cezanne*, Allgemeine Volkswirtschaftslehre, p. 154f.; *Cox/Jens/Markert*, Handbuch
des Wettbewerbs, p. 113f.; *Wied-Nebbeling*, Markt- und Preistheorie, 3. ed. 1997, p. 2.

ket form in favour of the undertaking considering the future development.[94]

In case of heterogeneous competition the behavioural scope of an undertaking reacting to the competitive situation allows for different marketing and competition strategies with best case and worst case scenarios. Only the internal business plans show whether the undertaking perceives undertakings close to the market, which can enter it due to their possibility to switch production, already as threat to its market position and whether it acts providently. No external economic analysis procedure (Cross Price Elasticity of demand, SSNIP-Test, Price Correlation Analysis)[95] is able to make a precise statement about the effects of possible market entries from an ex ante view. The management of the undertaking has to decide whether the supply-side substitutability of potential competitors is to be perceived as a threat to their own position and whether thus a provident reaction is necessary.

---

[94] Cf. *Cezanne* (supra n. 93), p. 155.

[95] Cf. the short description of the concepts used in price theory in *Klaue/Schwintowski*, Marktabgrenzung und Marktbeherrschung im Telekommunikationssektor, 2001, p. 32ff.; cf. *Schwalbe*, in: Münchener Kommentar zum europäischen und deutschen Wettbewerbsrecht (Kartellrecht), Bd. I, 2007, Intro. H para. 1155ff.; cf. also *Bishop/Walker*, The Economics of EC Competition, 2. ed. 2002, para. 8.01ff. (Part III).

Relevant market in terms of business plan concept

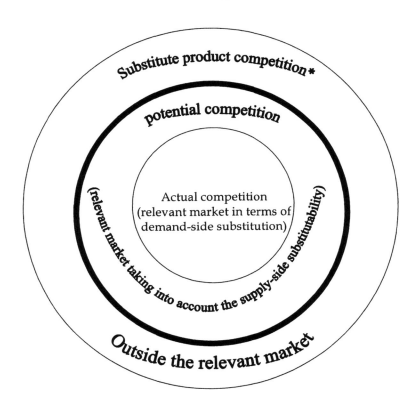

* Substitute product competition has to be taken into account not at the market definition stage but at the later stage of appraising the creation or strengthening of a dominant position. The consideration of subsitute product competition at this stage can lead to a negation of the dominant position, if in a realistic prognosis it is expected, that the buyers will in the unforeseeable future increasingly turn to substitute products close to the market. The same applies, if it is expected that the subsitute product competition will asymmetrically only effect singular competitive products in the relevant market.

The undertakings decide with their competitive strategies how wide the relevant market is. If they plan without taking into consideration undertakings capable of switching production and ready to enter the market, a non-competitive behaviour is to be expected. This is because not the objective-morphological criteria, but the consequences the undertakings derive from these criteria and use in their business plans determine the relevant market. This applies in particular to oligopolistic markets. An undertaking, which perceives competitors not as not limiting its behavioural margin, but instead counts e.g. on collusive behaviour in a narrow homogeneous and symmetrical oligopoly, may not invoke intensive competition in a cartel procedure. If an undertaking feels forced to act pro-competitively not only by demand-side substitution (concept of demand-side substitutability) but also by supply-side substitution, then it must prove the latter with the help of its marketing concept and the competitive strategies derived from it.

The concept of supply-side substitutability amends and extends the concept of demand-side substitutability. Without analysing the possibility to switch production the market cannot be correctly defined. The concept of demand-side substitutability only regards the pressure exerted from the current product preferences of the consumers without identifying the preferences empirically.[96] In comparison it seems more appropriate to consider the complex market evaluations of the undertakings, which are included in the business plans and which have been derived through an intense internal decision process. This does not open the floodgates to "fairy tales" and lies. If a pharmaceutical company argues that it feels pressured not only by seven other Benzodiazepam products, but also by 164 other sleeping pills, the cartel authorities and courts are able to evaluate such statement. Not the ex post statement before the court or au-

---

[96] The legal authorities applying the law determine the market according to their own knowledge, without presenting a poof for this knowledge; cf. BGH, WuW DE-R 1925, para. 15 - National Geographic II.

thority is decisive, but the ex ante business plan and the competitive strategy derived from it. Country specific international strategic business plans are the basis for future decisions and are used for reporting and counselling purposes in the supervisory board (§ 90(1) no. 2 German Stock Corporation Act – "Aktiengesetz"); they can thus be distinguished from a result-oriented presentation in the cartel procedure. This is in particular true as often neutral market studies exist, which have been produced without regard to a specific case. In case of big companies (with division of labor) it must not be feared that the undertakings write new marketing plans especially for the cartel procedure. Though these undertakings are not "moral institutions", they act in their self-interest, when they present correct plans according to the compliance rules in order to reach legal certainty (§ 40 (2) sentence 3 no. 2 German Competition Act) and to prevent infringement procedures.

The concept of business plans allows determining the competitive pressure directly through the perspective of the undertakings, which are exposed to it and must act accordingly. The necessity to act according to the current and future competitive constraints manifests itself in the daily actions of the undertakings as follows: As soon as a competitor offers a new product, which diminishes the demand for rival products, their suppliers need to react with price reductions, quality improvements or massive advertising. The same applies if a new rival product must be met with the development of an own, at least equivalent product in order not to lose market shares. Therefore, an undertaking, which is interested in a successful marketing of its products long term, will take into consideration in its business plan not only present, but also future competitors. It considers future competitors, which are able to adapt their production technically and financially in order to enter the relevant market should it be profitable.[97]

---

[97]　Cf. n. 38.

As the strategic business plan of the undertaking forecasts several years in the future, it provides a valuable advantage for Merger Control: The future competitive constraints are included in the business plan, if the merging parties believe that companies close to the market will extend their product range and enter the market. Although these constitute only future developments, the danger of a possible market entry already affects the present strategy. A company, which claims a market share of 70% over many years, e.g. on a market for a homogeneous product, is not always a monopolistic supplier. This is for example not the case, if price and quality of the products are determined by stock market prices[98] or by foreign competitors, who just wait for the chance to enter the domestic market should a price increase occur or to enter the market with a new technology.[99] If the prices remain consistently low in order to hinder a possible entry of a competitor, there is no reason to doubt the intensity of potential competition.

Furthermore, the business plan takes into consideration expected changes in *demand behaviour*. Should readers for instance increasingly use electronic publications as alternative to the print media, then traditional media products compete with electronic media products. The fact that publishing companies have to consider these future consequences already today in their business plan in order to prevent dramatically reduced turnovers in future years is obvious. Hence, already the marketing plan of today shows how the market will develop in the future from the view of the undertaking. The concept of business plans is therefore a systematically necessary correction of the concept of demand-side substitutability, with the purpose of including the aspect of supply-side substitutability and potential competition. While the concept of demand-side substitutability is limited to the assessment of whether other products are

---

[98] BGH, WuW/E BGH 1824, 1827 Tonolli/Blei- and Silberhütte Braubach.
[99] Federal Cartel Office (BKartA), Tätigkeitsbericht 1981/1982, p. 106 („Mannesmann/Kienzle").

currently functionally interchangeable to cover the same demand, the concept of supply-side substitutability makes sure that the specific competitive constraints and thus the width of the relevant product market are defined with the help of the marketing plan of the undertakings.[100]

---

[100] The Federal Cartel Office (B4-107 / 00 [Richemont-LMH]) defined for examples for watches a market on the basis of the concept of demand-side substitutability, which is differentiated according to the price (over 10000 German Mark). However, subjective preferences of many consumers concerning exclusivity, tradition or special prestige would have lead by considering the undertakings' business plans to a separate market for watches of the so-called "Haute Horlogerie" standard. In this case the Geneva top-selling mass manufacturer would, as a market outsider, not have been able to balance out the market power of the merging undertakings. A supplier will take stable subjective preferences as serious as an objectively given functional interchangeability, if a significant number of customers attach importance not so much to the robustness and accuracy of the watch, but rather to a traditional (luxurious) brand with a distinctive and prestigious optic. Considering the business plan will thus not always lead to a broadening of the market definition.

C. Determining the relevant market according to the marketing plan – Examples

That the market determination according to the business plans of the undertakings is appropriate will be shown in the following with the case studies introduced above.

As various decisions show the cartel authorities have recognised the necessity to correct the concept of demand-side substitutability. Presently the Federal Cartel Office alludes to a "modified concept of demand-side substitutability".[101] Determining markets only from the perspective of the consumer does not lead, as the examples have shown, to an appropriate consideration of the competitive relations as in all mentioned cases a certain clothes size, screw, trip or professional publication is not interchangeable with another for the consumer. A strict application of the concept of demand-side substitutability would have resulted in splitting of the concerned markets in dozens of small markets. The Commission and the Federal Cartel Office leave it unclear how the specific *demand* is defined for which the concept of demand-side substitutability determines the functional interchangeability. It is unrealistic to assume that the consumer, looking for professional publications, a certain clothes size or a certain tool or spice, just wants any professional publication, spice, clothes or tool. Vice versa it would go too far to demand a *full* functional interchangeability.[102] This would reduce the concept of demand-side substitutability to absurdity. If one defined the demand of the normal consumer as the search for a specific garment or a specific book of a specific poet, then the garment of company

---

[101] B6-104/99 [only partially published in WuW/E DE-V 191ff.; in full length on the homepage: http://www.bundeskartellamt.de] (The case concerned the acquisition of all company shares of the Nomos-Verlag through the publisher Verlag C. H. Beck; seller was the publisher Springer-Wissenschaftsverlag). The criteria of modification remain vague.

[102] Federal Cartel Office, 21.06.2000, B 10 - 25/00 - Melitta Bentz/Schultink; Federal Cartel Office, 04.05.2004, B 3 - 154/03 - Colgate/Gaba, para. 34; Commission, 15.02.1999, Case no. M. 1377, para. 10 – Bertelsmann/ Wissenschaftsverlag Springer.

XY or the specific best-seller would each form an independent market. Other products of the same type would – at the most – be substitute goods. The average customer is willing to consider another garment with the same purpose or another travel destination in the same region or another manual with the same topic. The concept of demand-side substitutability would define the market narrower than the competitive constraints suggest. Even if the consumers' demand is interpreted in a wide way, the concept of demand-side substitutability would create only a market for family law books, for blue jeans, for pepper, for hammers etc. In no case would a "modified" market for men's wear, spices, manuals for professional or non-professional legal users, tools as such be created. Only if the supply-side substitutability is considered in these cases, a wider market definition is justified, if the business plans of the undertakings involved show that the undertakings are influenced by the flexibility of potential competitors to switch production.

In the merger case Beck/Nomos the Federal Cartel Office has assumed such influence.[103] The FCO held that the ability of the publishing companies "to align their production on the different business sectors in the area of professional/technical information" was decisive for the market definition. The requirements on the respective capabilities of the publishing companies stipulated by the Federal Cartel Office were low. The publishing companies only had to possess the ability to change production *in a short term* and *without problems*. The Federal Cartel Office found that this ability to switch production existed as a result of common "key competences" within the "business segment of law books". It mentioned knowledge, reputation, distribution channels and author relations as belonging to the key competences. By doing so it defined the market widely as market for law information for professional and non-professional legal users. It did not even allow to divide the book market for pro-

---

[103] Ibid., para. 7.

fessional users into segments for the different areas of law. Instead it dismissed such fragmentation arguing that with regard to the insofar existing supply-side substitutability this would be "arbitrary".[104] The concept of demand-side substitutability has thus been obviously abandoned.

However, in the case B6-88/00[105] the Federal Cartel Office applied the classic concept of demand-side substitutability without disputing the question in which cases which of the concepts is to be applied. According to the Federal Cartel Office separate markets exist for fishing and hunting magazines. It only considered the different consumer preferences by contrasting the interest on *exclusively* fishing with the interest on *exclusively* hunting.[106] This narrow market definition conflicts with the case "Beck/Nomos". In this case the consumers depended professionally on specific information thus deserving the protection of the concept of demand-side substitutability more than the hobby fisher or hunter.[107]

The „Beck-Nomos" decision has become less absolute with the decision of the Federal Cartel Office in the case B6-56/01 from 22. August 2001,[108] which also dealt with publications for professional users. Here the Federal Cartel Office again affirmed the concurrence of the concept of demand-side substitutability and the concept of supply-side substitutability.[109] It also considered the business plans of

---

[104] Ibid., para. 8.
[105] The case concerned the formation of a joint venture two publishers, both publishing fishing and hunting magazines.
[106] Ibid., para. 7.
[107] This conflicts with the wide market definition of package air travels. Here neither destination nor main interests are considered, but only the supply-side substitutability.
[108] The case concerned the acquisition of among others professional journals on electronics through a publisher already publishing such journals (SV-C Verwaltungs GmbH / WEKA).
[109] Ibid., para. 9, 11.

the undertakings involved[110] by looking at the relevant consumer groups the publishers had in mind when designing their magazines.[111] The Federal Cartel Office thus formed separate markets for professional publications concerning the use of electronics in end user products and professional publications dealing with the use of electronics in manufacturing processes. This result is different to that stipulated in the case „Beck-Nomos", where the Federal Cartel Office did not consider different consumer groups. According to the ratio decidendi in the cases B6-88/00 and B6-56/01 the Federal Cartel Office should have assumed separate markets also in "Beck/Nomos" – i.e. a separate market for each area of law.

Also in the case of other consumer goods and services (clothes, food, beverages, leisure and business trips, radio broadcast and television shows) and capital goods (tools, parts, equipment) the concept of demand-side substitutability results in too narrow market determinations, which do not adequately show the constraints of current and potential competition, to which the undertakings are exposed. This is the case if the concept is applied according to its heuristic objective as ex ante instrument for the appropriate empiric market determination and not modified as empty ex post legitimisation formula. According to the concept of demand-side substitutability each clothes or screw size, each spice or each tea, each travel destination and each vacuum cleaner bag[112] forms according to the subjective demand of the consumer a separate product market, as the products are not functionally, i.e. according to their intended use, interchangeable. The result is a mislead competition policy. In all these cases the concept of demand-side substitutability only de-fines the individual consumer demands, but it does not deliver a criterion to aggregate the consumer demands in an abstract way on the level on which the competition between the undertakings takes place. In

---

[110] Ibid., para. 16f.
[111] Ibid., para. 21.
[112] Each vacuum cleaner needs special bags, which cannot be used for other brands.

contrast the criterion of supply-side substitutability defines exactly the "field", on which the competitive constraints are effective.

The aspect of supply-side substitutability played the decisive role in the Commission decision „Bertelsmann-Wissenschaftsverlag/ Springer".[113] As this decision shows, in the case of professional publications not only the German, but also the European cartel authority have abandoned the concept of demand-side substitutability and instead taken into account the capability of the publishing companies to switch production (supply-side substitutability). Though the Commission emphasises that the starting point for defining the market is the *concept of demand-side substitutability*, it finds it at the same time "inappropriate" (similar to the Federal Cartel Office in "Beck-Nomos") as it is not suitable to show the existing competitive relations between the undertakings and the effects of the merger on competition.[114] Determining markets according to the interchangeability between the specific products would lead to an "immense number" of small markets;[115] and thus the competitive constraints would not be sufficiently registered.[116]

When assessing the *supply-side substitutability* the Commission rightly asked, which requirements an undertaking must meet in order to be considered a supplier for professional publications. Similar to the Federal Cartel Office[117] the Commission mentioned the factors reputation, access to authors and editors, knowledge of the customer basis and distribution channels.[118] But the question how long it would take to realise the switching of production was not

---

[113] OJ 1999 C 122: a uniform market for academic and professional publications of each subject.
[114] Ibid., para. 9.
[115] Examples of the Commission: Medicine / Law; within the customer category „Law": publications on income tax/ publications on turnover tax.
[116] Ibid., para. 10.
[117] Cf. B6-104/99 „Beck - Nomos", para. 8.
[118] Ibid., para. 11.

explicitly mentioned by the Commission. As professional authors do not have unprinted manuscripts in stock and are also not able to produce a rival product at short notice, the relevant market cannot be extended offhand on grounds of supply-side substitutability. What is also not very convincing is the Commission's argument that universities and other research institutes demand scientific publications by bundle.[119] To base the market definition on such undifferentiated demand contradicts the concept of functional interchangeability. Many consumers carry a whole "bundle" of food home after shopping. Still, this would not cause anyone to determine a uniform "food market" ("Everything what a man/woman can eat or drink"). The same applies to the market for publications ("Everything what a man/woman can read") and the markets for manuals or law books – such uniform markets do not exist. An energy lawyer does not need a book on criminal law, a cardiologist does not need a textbook on gynaecology. A product market does not expand merely because some consumers buy a bundle of products in order to give them other consumers to use. The suppliers only care for winning as many users as possible, because this is the only reason why products are put on the market and, if necessary, sold in bundles. Without readers being interested in the specific books, libraries would be useless and no buyers would exist. To justify its conclusion the Commission also relies on the appraisal of the undertakings involved,[120] but it does not make clear according to which criteria the ability to switch production is considered. However, the methodical approach to start from the marketing strategies of the undertakings involved and to consider the assessment expressed in them about which undertakings the publishing company regards as its current and potential competitors, is correct.

The merger control procedure of *Gruner&Jahr/Zeit* showed how realistic a business plan of an undertaking depicts the relevant prod-

---

[119] Ibid., para. 11.
[120] Cf. ibid., para. 11.

uct market. The Federal Cartel Office[121] determined a market for weekly newspapers, including *Vorwärts, Rheinischer Merkur, Bildwoche* and *Zeit*. Gräfin Dönhoff and Gerd Bucerius (editors of the *Zeit*) stated as witnesses (and proved with examples) that the only real competition for the *Zeit* were the nationwide daily newspapers like *FAZ* and *Süddeutsche*. These newspapers have six issues per week to cover all topics in special reports, which the *Zeit* must fit into only one edition per week. As the readers of the *Zeit* can not do without a sophisticated daily newspaper to get the up-to-date daily news, there is always the danger, that they regard the *Zeit* as unnecessary and unsubscribe from it. Every increase in price led to a decrease in subscriptions. The business plan of the *Zeit* took into account only the *FAZ* and the *Süddeutsche Zeitung*. The cartel senate of the superior court of justice[122] found the market determination of the publishing company plausible after extensively appraising the evidence submitted. The senate found that the nationwide daily newspapers did exert strong competition pressure on the *Zeit*, but not on the other weekly papers and therefore annulled the prohibition decision of the Federal Cartel Office.[123]

The decisions show that the Federal Cartel Office and the European Commission are open to different methods for determining the market. If the application of the concept of demand-side substitutability results in too narrow markets, then they apply the concept of supply-side substitutability (Beck–Nomos / Bertelsmann–Wissen-

---

[121] BKartA, WuW/E FCO, 1863.
[122] Cf. KG, WuW/E OLG, 3807.
[123] The cartel-senate of the German Federal High Court (BGH, WuW/E BGH, 2112, 2113f. Gruner&Jahr/Zeit I, see also BGH, WuW/E BGH, 2433 Gruner&Jahr 2433 Gruner&Jahr Zeit II) annulled the decision of the Superior court of justice ("KG") as the decision did not explicitly stated that the competitive pressure, which exerted from FAZ and Süddeutsche Zeitung, would only affect the Zeit and not also other weekly papers. The more obvious something is, the less it is explicitly said, as the numerous implied declarations of intent exemplify; it is nevertheless tacitly (implicitly) said.

schaftsverlag Springer). In contrast, if smaller markets seem alluring (e.g. for instant meals without Ravioli,[124] instant soups and frozen instant meals[125] or hunting magazines) the concept of sup-ply-side substitutability is not mentioned. The limitations of the concept of demand-side substitutability become thus obvious. Only the concept of business plans guarantees a coherent and systematic registration of the competitive pressure exerted by present and potential competitors; this is because the business plans consider not only the aspect of demand substitution but also the supply-side substitutability (i.e. the ability to switch production). The product strategies expressed in the business plans provide the basis for reacting to competitive constraints, which affect the undertaking probably presently and in the future. Using the internal business plans as a starting point with significantly more incomplete information is more efficient from the point of competition theory and competition policy than to define the relevant market from outside.

In the practice of the competition authorities the concept of the business plans has not been accepted yet. This is because the practicability of the concept is doubted.[126] Some see a problem with the reliability of the competition data contained in the business plan. As shown above (B.2.c)aa)), these doubts are not justified. Business plans and the preceding marketing studies are not specially and result-oriented made for the respective competition authority; rather,

---

[124] Cf. BKartA, WuW/E, 1817, in contrast the superior court (WuW/E OLG, 3759, 3760f. - Pillsbury/Sonnen-Bassermann) put the Ravioli cans into the same relevant market. See also KG, WuW/E OLG 2403 - Fertigfutter.

[125] The Federal Cartel Office has not sufficiently considered that the more expansive frozen foods limit the scope of action of the suppliers of instant meals in cans and reduce the price. Thus, in my opinion, it was not correct to define an isolated market for instant meals.

[126] Cf. *Möschel*, in: Immenga/Mestmäcker, Kommentar zum Kartellgesetz, § 19, para. 32.

they are the basis for long-term and far reaching decisions, which can be requested without the risk of falsification.[127]

The *marketing strategy* of the undertaking provides information on which products the undertaking considers to be in competition to its own products. By doing so it reflects the demand market. However, the marketing strategy behind the business plan also reveals whether the undertaking believes that it soon has to adapt to new products: If it limits itself to advertising its own products, it does not expect that undertakings close to the market will enter its market. In contrast, if it actively engages in research and development in order to be able to react with its own new products, then potential competition seems to exist. §§ 57 ff. German Competition Act and Art. 11 ff. ECMR provide the respective competition authorities with the means to get the business plan – if necessary, by way of state instruments.

---

[127] *Scheuerle*, AcP 167 (1967), 305ff. regarding such final interpretations and their limits.

D. Summary

The purpose of defining markets is to differentiate competitive markets from markets in which the regulating hand of the state is indispensable. Every state intervention into effectively working competition processes would be a disproportionate intervention into the basic rights (Art. 2 and 12 German Constitution). To avoid excessive state interference a correct determination of the border between freedom of competition and market dominance is necessary. The classic concept of demand-side substitutability does not fulfil this purpose, as the determination according to the specific demand of the consumer will lead to atomised small markets.

A too narrow market definition can prevent effective competition from evolving for all market participants under the same conditions, if the real field of competition is wider than assumed by the competition authority. This is because a too narrow market determination labels an undertaking as market dominant; as a consequence this undertaking can not act the same way as undertakings can act which are assumed to act on the "substitution product market" but in reality are on the same market as the undertaking. This applies to structural measures (with regard to Art. 3 ECMR, § 36 German Competition Act) and competitive behaviour (Art. 81 EC, §§ 19, 20 German Competition Act). A too broad market determination may provide an undertaking, which in fact is market dominant, with a too large behavioural margin in case of mergers and product strategies, which increase its winning margin even further.

The "pure" application of the concept of demand-side substitutability leads to results that competition policy cannot accept and is thus useless. The concept of demand-side substitutability needs to be supplemented – not exceptionally and according to rather apocryptic criteria like it has been done so far, but systematically by structurally including the competition perspective. The consumer analysis must be extended by a competitor analysis, since the concept of demand-side substitutability records the consumer's wishes only statically in form of a snapshot without being able to take into consideration that these in fact are subject to permanent change. The static snapshot cannot properly capture the constant dynamic change in the consumer preferences, which is caused by new information and new advertising measures. In contrast, a realistic marketing strategy to optimise market share always also includes potential competitors. Market entry decisions as key decisions of the strategic economic planning, new positioning of products or price changes as operational marketing decisions are always based on thorough analysis. The undertaking distinguishes here between consumer goods marketing, capital goods marketing, commercial marketing and service marketing. To ignore the complex decision-making process of the strategic and operational marketing management, which is reflected in the product range policy, the communication policy, the price policy and the distribution policy of the undertaking, would be a big mistake. In order to place the evaluations around the issue of market dominance on a realistic fundament a theory is needed which equally considers supply- and demand-side substitutability.

A realistic market determination has to consider those undertakings as participants of the same relevant product market, which are taken into consideration by the competitors in their business plans and which limit their scope of action in particular to pricing. This is why the business plans of the undertakings must be the starting point for defining the market. The business plans reflect the objective-morphological market structure, with which the undertakings are confronted in the economic reality (if it is not one of the often discussed cases in which the undertaking is mistaken). The undertaking does not only consider as relevant competing products the products of undertakings, to which the consumer can switch his demand (actual competition), but also the products of undertakings, which are able to switch production short-term to products, which the consumer regards as functionally interchangeable with the products already in the market (potential competition). This is documented by the examples in footnotes 2 to 8. If one aims at a realistic – and not speculative – competition analysis, the starting point has to be the relevant market as defined by the business plans of the undertakings.

Especially in the case of merger control the concept of business plan is more effective than the concept of demand-side substitutability – while the former considers not only the actual competition caused by the ability of the consumer to switch to another product, but also the potential competition expected in the future, which results from the ability to switch production; the latter ignores the competitive pressure caused by potential competitors willing to enter the market. The products of the potential competitors are to be included in the relevant market. Thus the relevant market changes from a pep-per to a spice market, from a market for travels to Greece to a market for travels in warm Mediterranean countries, from a market for fishing magazines to a market for hobby magazines, from a golf class market to a market for passenger cars. This normally leads to smaller market shares, which reflect the importance of potential competition for limiting the behavioural scope of the undertaking on the market. Thereby the competition law provisions, which are based on market shares (§ 19(3) German Competition Act, Art. 3 Vertical Agreements Block Exemption), regain their importance in signalling actual threats to competition.

Appendix I[1]: Commission Notice on the definition of the relevant market for the purposes of Community competition law.

(Only the published text is authentic. Published in the Official Journal: OJ C 372 on 9/12/1997)

I.   Introduction

1. The purpose of this notice is to provide guidance as to how the Commission applies the concept of relevant product and geographic market in its ongoing enforcement of Community competition law, in particular the application of Regulations 17/62 and 4064/89, their equivalents in other sectoral applications such as transport, coal and steel, and agriculture, and the relevant provisions of the EEA agreement.[2] Throughout this notice, references to Articles 85 and 86 of the Treaty and to merger control are to be understood as referring to the equivalent provisions in the EEA agreement and the ECSC Treaty.

2. Market definition is a tool to identify and define the boundaries of competition between firms. It allows to establish the framework within which competition policy is applied by the Commission. The main purpose of market definition is to identify in a systematic way the competitive constraints that the undertakings involved[3] face. The objective of defining a market in both its product and geo-

---

[1]   Today, Art. 85 and 86 are Art. 81 and 82; EC-Regulation No. 17/62 is now No. 1/2003 and No. 4064/89 is now No. 139/2004.

[2]   The focus of assessment in state aid cases is the aid recipient and the industry/sector concerned rather than identification of competitive constraints faced by the aid recipient. When consideration of market power and therefore of the relevant market are raised in any particular case, elements of the approach outlined here might serve as a basis for the assessment of state aid cases.

[3]   For the purposes of this notice, the undertakings involved will be in the case of a concentration the parties to the concentration. In investigations under Article 86 of the Treaty, the undertaking being investigated or the complainants. For investigations under Article 85, the parties to the agreement.

graphic dimension is to identify those actual competitors of the undertakings involved that are capable of constraining their behaviour and of preventing them from behaving independently of an effective competitive pressure. It is from this perspective, that the market definition makes it possible, *inter alia*, to calculate market shares that would convey meaningful information regarding market power for the purposes of assessing dominance or for the purposes of applying Article 85.

3. It follows from the above, that the concept of relevant market is different from other concepts of market often used in other contexts. For instance, companies often use the term market to refer to the area where it sells its products or to refer broadly to the industry or sector where it belongs.

4. The definition of the relevant market in both its product and geographic dimensions often has a decisive influence on the assessment of a competition case. By rendering public the procedures the Commission follows when considering market definition and by indicating the criteria and evidence on which it relies to reach a decision, the Commission expects to increase the transparency of its policy and decision making in the area of competition policy.

5. Increased transparency will also result in companies and their advisors being able to better anticipate the possibility that the Commission would raise competition concerns in an individual case. Companies could, therefore, take such a possibility into account in their own internal decision making when contemplating for instance, acquisitions, the creation of joint ventures or the establishment of certain agreements. It is also intended that companies are in a better position to understand what sort of information the Commission considers relevant for the purposes of market definition.

6. The Commission's interpretation of the notion of relevant market is without prejudice to the interpretation which may be given by the Court of Justice or the Court of First Instance of the European Communities.

II.   Definition of relevant market

Definition of relevant product and relevant geographic market

7. The regulations based on Articles 85 and 86 of the Treaty, in particular in section 6 of Form A/B with respect to Regulation 17, as well as in section 6 of Form CO with respect to regulation 4064/89 on the control of concentrations of a Community dimension have laid down the following definitions. Relevant product markets are defined as follows:

"A relevant product market comprises all those products and/or services which are regarded as interchangeable or substitutable by the consumer, by reason of the products' characteristics, their prices and their intended use."

8. Relevant geographic markets are defined as follows:

"The relevant geographic market comprises the area in which the undertakings concerned are involved in the supply and demand of products or services, in which the conditions of competition are sufficiently homogeneous and which can be distinguished from neighbouring areas because the conditions of competition are appreciably different in those areas".

9. The relevant market within which to assess a given competition issue is therefore established by the combination of the product and geographic markets. The Commission interprets the definitions at paragraphs 7 and 8 (which reflect the jurisprudence of the Court of Justice and the Court of First Instance as well as its own decisional practice) according to the orientations defined in this Notice.

Concept of relevant market and objectives of Community competition policy

10. The concept of relevant market is closely related to the objectives pursued under Community competition policy. For example under the Community's merger control, the objective in controlling structural changes in the supply of a product/service is to prevent the creation or reinforcement of a dominant position as a result of

which effective competition would be significantly impeded in a substantial part of the common market. Under the Community's competition policy, a dominant position is such that a firm or group of firms would be in a position to behave to an appreciable extent independently of its competitors, customers and ultimately of its consumers.[4] Such a position would usually arise when a firm or group of firms would account for a large share of the supply in any given market, provided that other factors analysed in the assessment (such as entry barriers, capacity of reaction of customers, etc.) point in the same direction.

11. The same approach is followed by the Commission in its application of Article 86 of the Treaty to firms that enjoy a single or collective dominant position. Under Regulation 17 the Commission has the power to investigate and bring to an end abuses of such a dominant position, which must also be defined by reference to the relevant market. Markets may also need to be defined in the application of Article 85 of the Treaty, in particular, in determining whether an appreciable restriction of competition exists or in establishing if the condition under Article 85 (3) b) for an exemption from the application of article 85(1) is met.

12. The criteria to define the relevant market are applied generally for the analysis of certain behaviours in the market and for the analysis of structural changes in the supply of products. This methodology, though, might lead to different results depending on the nature of the competition issue being examined. For instance, the scope of the geographic market might be different when analysing a concentration, where the analysis is essentially prospective, than when analysing past behaviour. The different time horizon considered in each case might lead to the result that different geographic markets are defined for the same products depending on whether

---

4   Definition given by the Court of Justice in Hoffmann La Roche (CJEC Sentence of 13.02.1979, case 85/76), and confirmed in subsequent judgements.

the Commission is examining a change in the structure of supply, such as a concentration or a cooperative joint venture, or issues relating to certain past behaviour.

Basic principles for market definition

Competitive constraints

13. Firms are subject to three main sources of competitive constraints: demand substitutability, supply substitutability and potential competition. From an economic point of view, for the definition of the relevant market, demand substitution constitutes the most immediate and effective disciplinary force on the suppliers of a given product, in particular in relation to their pricing decisions. A firm or a group of firms cannot have a significant impact on the prevailing conditions of sale, such as prices, if its customers are in a position to switch easily to available substitute products or to suppliers located elsewhere. Basically, the exercise of market definition consists in identifying the effective alternative sources of supply for the customers of the undertakings involved, both in terms of products/services and geographic location of suppliers.

14. The competitive constraints arising from supply side substitutability other then those described in paragraphs 20 to 23 and from potential competition are in general less immediate and in any case require an analysis of additional factors. As a result such constraints are taken into account at the assessment stage of competition analysis.

Demand substitution

15. The assessment of demand substitution entails a determination of the range of products which are viewed as substitutes by the consumer. One way of making this determination can be viewed, as a thought experiment, postulating a hypothetical small, non-transitory change in relative prices and evaluating the likely reactions of customers to that increase. The exercise of market definition focuses on prices for operational and practical purposes, and more precisely on demand substitution arising from small, permanent

changes in relative prices. This concept can provide clear indications as to the evidence that is relevant to define markets.

16. Conceptually, this approach implies that starting from the type of products that the undertakings involved sell and the area in which they sell them, additional products and areas will be included into or excluded from the market definition depending on whether competition from these other products and areas affect or restrain sufficiently the pricing of the parties' products in the short term.

17. The question to be answered is whether the parties' customers would switch to readily available substitutes or to suppliers located elsewhere in response to an hypothetical small (in the range 5%-10%), permanent relative price increase in the products and areas being considered. If substitution would be enough to make the price increase unprofitable because of the resulting loss of sales, additional substitutes and areas are included in the relevant market. This would be done until the set of products and geographic areas is such that small, permanent increases in relative prices would be profitable. The equivalent analysis is applicable in cases concerning the concentration of buying power, where the starting point would then be the supplier and the price test allows to identify the alternative distribution channels or outlets for the supplier's products. In the application of these principles, careful account should be taken of certain particular situations as described under paragraphs 56 and 58.

18. A practical example of this test can be provided by its application to a merger of, for instance, soft drink bottlers. An issue to examine in such a case would be to decide whether different flavours of soft drinks belong to the same market. In practice, the question to ad-dress would be if consumers of flavour A would switch to other flavours when confronted with a permanent price increase of 5% to 10% for flavour A. If a sufficient number of consumers would switch to, say, flavour B, to such an extent that the price increase for flavour A would not be profitable due to the resulting loss of sales,

then the market would comprise at least flavours A and B. The process would have to be extended in addition to other available flavours until a set of products is identified for which a price rise would not induce a sufficient substitution in demand.

19. Generally, and in particular for the analysis of merger cases, the price to take into account will be the prevailing market price. This might not be the case where the prevailing price has been determined in the absence of sufficient competition. In particular for investigation of abuses of dominant positions, the fact that the prevailing price might already have been substantially increased will be taken into account.

Supply substitution

20. Supply-side substitutability may also be taken into account when defining markets in those situations in which its effects are equivalent to those of demand substitution in terms of effectiveness and immediacy. This requires that suppliers be able to switch production to the relevant products and market them in the short term[5] without incurring significant additional costs or risks in response to small and permanent changes in relative prices. When these conditions are met, the additional production that is put on the market will have a disciplinary effect on the competitive behaviour of the companies involved. Such an impact in terms of effectiveness and immediacy is equivalent to the demand substitution effect.

21. These situations typically arise when companies market a wide range of qualities or grades of one product; even if for a given final customer or group of consumers, the different qualities are not substitutable, the different qualities will be grouped into one product market provided that most of the suppliers are able to offer and sell the various qualities under the conditions of immediacy and ab-

---

[5]   I.e. the period which does not imply a significant adjustment of existing tangible and intangible assets (see para 23).

sence of significant increase in costs described above. In such cases, the relevant product market will encompass all products that are substitutable in demand and supply, and the current sales of those products will be summed to calculate the total value or volume of the market. The same reasoning may lead to group different geographic areas.

22. A practical example of the approach to supply side substitutability when defining product markets is to be found in the case of paper. Paper is usually supplied in a range of different qualities, from standard writing paper to high quality papers to be used for instance to publish art books. From a demand point of view, different qualities of paper cannot be used for a specific use, i.e. an art book or a high quality publication cannot be based on lower quality papers. However, paper plants are prepared to manufacture the different qualities, and production can be adjusted with negligible costs and in a short time frame. In the absence of particular difficulties in distribution, paper manufacturers are able therefore to compete for orders of the various qualities, in particular if orders are passed with a sufficient lead time to allow to modify production plans. Under such circumstances, the Commission would not define a separate market for each quality of paper and respective usage. The various qualities of paper are included in the relevant market, and their sales added up to estimate total market value and volume.

23. When supply side substitutability would imply the need to adjust significantly existing tangible and intangible assets, additional in-vestments, strategic decisions or time delays, it will not be considered at the stage of market definition. Examples where supply side substitution did not lead the Commission to enlarge the market are offered in the area of consumer products, in particular for branded beverages. Although bottling plants may in principle bottle different beverages, there are costs and lead times involved (in terms of advertising, product testing and distribution) before the products can actually be sold. In these cases, the effects of supply

side substitutability and other forms of potential competition would then be examined at a later stage.

Potential competition

24. The third source of competitive constraint, potential competition, is not taken into account when defining markets, since the conditions under which potential competition will actually represent an effective competitive constraint depend on the analysis of specific factors and circumstances related to the conditions of entry. If required, this analysis is only carried out at a subsequent stage, in general once the position of the companies involved in the relevant market has already been ascertained, and such position is indicative of concerns from a competition point of view.

III. Evidence relied upon to define relevant markets

The process of defining the relevant market in practice.

Product dimension

25. There is a range of evidence permitting to assess the extent to which substitution would take place. In individual cases, certain types of evidence will be determinant, depending very much on the characteristics and specificity of the industry and products or services that are being examined. The same type of evidence may be of no importance in other cases. In most cases, a decision will have to be based on the consideration of a number of criteria and different items of evidence. The Commission follows an open approach to empirical evidence, aimed at making an effective use of all available information which may be relevant in individual cases. The Commission does not follow a rigid hierarchy of different sources of information or types of evidence.

26. The process of defining relevant markets may be summarised as follows: on the basis of the preliminary information available or information submitted by the undertakings involved, the Commission will usually be in a position to broadly establish the possible relevant markets within which, for instance a concentration or a restric-

tion of competition has to be assessed. In general, and for all practical purposes when handling individual cases, the question will usually be to decide on a few alternative possible relevant markets. For instance, with respect to the product market, the issue will often be to establish whether product A and product B belong or do not belong to the same product market. It is often the case that the inclusion of product B would be enough to remove any competition concerns.

27. In such situations it is not necessary to consider whether the market also includes additional products and reach a definitive conclusion on the precise product market. If under the conceivable alternative market definitions the operation in question does not raise competition concerns, the question of market definition will be left open, reducing thereby the burden on companies to supply information.

Geographic dimension

28. The Commission's approach to geographic market definition might be summarised as follows: it will take a preliminary view of the scope of the geographic market on the basis of broad indications regarding the distribution of market shares of the parties and their competitors as well as a preliminary analysis of pricing and price differences at national and EU or EEA level. This initial view is used basically as a working hypothesis to focus the Commission's enquiries for the purposes of arriving at a precise geographic market definition.

29. The reasons behind any particular configuration of prices and market shares need to be explored. Companies might enjoy high market shares in their domestic markets just because of the weight of the past, and conversely, a homogeneous presence of companies throughout the EEA might be consistent with national or regional geographic markets. The initial working hypothesis will therefore be checked against an analysis of demand characteristics (importance of national or local preferences, current patterns of purchases of customers, product differentiation/brands, other) in order to es-

tablish whether companies in different areas do really constitute an actual alternative source of supply for consumers. The theoretical experiment is again based on substitution arising from changes in relative prices, and the question to answer is again whether the customers of the parties would switch their orders to companies located elsewhere in the short term and at a negligible cost.

30. If necessary, a further check on supply factors will be carried out to ensure that those companies located in distinct areas do not face impediments to develop their sales on competitive terms throughout the whole geographic market. This analysis will include an examination of requirements for a local presence in order to sell in that area, the conditions of access to distribution channels, costs associated with setting up a distribution network, and the existence or absence of regulatory barriers arising from public procurement, price regulations, quotas and tariffs limiting trade or production, technical standards, monopolies, freedom of establishment, requirements for administrative authorisations, packaging regulations, etc. In short, the Commission will identify possible obstacles and barriers isolating companies located in a given area from the competitive pressure of companies located outside that area, so as to determine the precise degree of market interpenetration at national, European or global level.

31. The actual pattern and evolution of trade flows offers useful supplementary indications as to the economic importance of each demand or supply factors mentioned above, and the extent to which they may or may not constitute actual barriers creating different geographic markets. The analysis of trade flows will generally address the question of transport costs and the extent to which these may hinder trade between different areas, having regard to plant location, costs of production and relative price levels.

Market integration in the European Union
32. Finally, the Commission also takes into account the continuing process of market integration in particular in the European Union when defining geographic markets, especially in the area of concen-

trations and structural joint ventures. The measures adopted and implemented in the internal market programme to remove barriers to trade and further integrate the community markets cannot be ignored when assessing the effects on competition of a concentration or a structural joint venture. A situation where national markets have been artificially isolated from each other because of the existence of legislative barriers that have now been removed, will generally lead to a cautious assessment of past evidence regarding prices, market shares or trade patterns. A process of market integration that would, in the short term, lead to wider geographic markets may therefore be taken into consideration when defining the geographic market for the purposes of assessing concentrations and joint ventures.

The process of gathering evidence

33. When a precise market definition is deemed necessary, the Commission will often contact the main customers and the main companies in the industry to enquire into their views about the boundaries of product and geographic markets and to obtain the necessary factual evidence to reach a conclusion. The Commission might also contact the relevant professional associations, and where appropriate, companies active in upstream markets, so as to be able to define, insofar as necessary, separate product and geographic markets, for different levels of production or distribution of the products/services in question. It might also request additional information to the undertakings involved.

34. Where appropriate, the Commission services will address written requests for information to the market players mentioned above. These requests will usually include questions relating to the perceptions of companies about reactions to hypothetical price increases and their views of the boundaries of the relevant market. They will also include requests to provide the factual information the Commission deems necessary to reach a conclusion on the extent of the relevant market. The Commission services might also discuss with marketing directors or other officers of those companies to gain a

better understanding on how negotiations between suppliers and customers take place and better understand issues relating to the definition of the relevant market. Where appropriate, they might also carry out visits or inspections to the premises of the parties, their customers and/or their competitors, in order to better understand how products are manufactured and sold.

35. The type of evidence relevant to reach a conclusion as to the product market can be categorised as follows.

Evidence to define markets - product dimension.

36. An analysis of the product characteristics and its intended use al-lows the Commission, in a first step, to limit the field of investigation of possible substitutes. However, product characteristics and intended use are insufficient to conclude whether two products are demand substitutes. Functional interchangeability or similarity in characteristics may not provide in themselves sufficient criteria because the responsiveness of customers to relative price changes may be determined by other considerations also. For example, there may be different competitive constraints in the original equipment market for car components and in spare parts, thereby leading to a distinction of two relevant markets. Conversely, differences in product characteristics are not in themselves sufficient to exclude demand substitutability, since this will depend to a large extent on how customers value different characteristics.

37. The type of evidence the Commission considers relevant to assess whether two products are demand substitutes can be categorised as follows:

38. *Evidence of substitution in the recent past.* In certain cases, it is possible to analyse evidence relating to recent past events or shocks in the market that offer actual examples of substitution between two products. When available, this sort of information will normally be fundamental for market definition. If there have been changes in relative prices in the past (all else being equal), the reactions in terms of quantities demanded will be determinant in establishing substitutability. Launches of new products in the past can also offer

useful information, when it is possible to precisely analyse which products lost sales to the new product.

39. There are a number of *quantitative* tests that have specifically been designed for the purpose of delineating markets. These tests consist of various econometric and statistical approaches: estimates of elasticities and cross-price elasticities[6] for the demand of a product, tests based on similarity of price movements over time, the analysis of causality between price series and similarity of price levels and/or their convergence. The Commission takes into account the available quantitative evidence capable of withstanding rigorous scrutiny for the purposes of establishing patterns of substitution in the past.

40. *Views of customers and competitors*. The Commission often contacts the main customers and competitors of the companies involved in its enquiries, to gather their views on the boundaries of the product market as well as most of the factual information it requires to reach a conclusion on the scope of the market. Reasoned answers of customers and competitors as to what would happen if relative prices for the candidate products would increase in the candidate geographic area by a small amount (for instance of 5%-10%) are taken into account when they are sufficiently backed by factual evidence.

41. *Consumer preferences*. In cases of consumer goods, it might be difficult for the Commission to gather the direct views of end consumers about substitute products. *Marketing studies* that companies have commissioned in the past and that are used by companies in their own decision making as to pricing of their products and/or marketing actions may provide useful information for the Commission's

---

6   Own price elasticity of demand for product X is a measure of the responsiveness of demand for X to percentage change in its own price. Cross-price elasticity between products X and Y is the responsiveness of demand for product X to percentage change in the price of product Y.

delineation of the relevant market. Consumer surveys on usage patterns and attitudes, data from consumer's purchasing patterns, the views expressed by retailers and more generally, market research studies submitted by the parties and their competitors are taken into account to establish whether an economically significant proportion of consumers consider two products as substitutable, taking also into account the importance of brands for the products in question. The methodology followed in consumer surveys carried out *ad-hoc* by the undertakings involved or their competitors for the purposes of a merger procedure or a procedure under Regulation 17 will usually be scrutinized with utmost care. Unlike pre-existing studies, they have not been prepared in the normal course of business for the adoption of business decisions.

42. *Barriers and costs associated with switching demand to potential substitutes.* There are a number of barriers and costs that might prevent the Commission from considering two *prima facie* demand substitutes as belonging to one single product market. It is not possible to provide an exhaustive list of all the possible barriers to substitution and of switching costs. These barriers or obstacles might have a wide range of origins, and in its decisions, the Commission has been confronted with regulatory barriers or other forms of State intervention, constraints arising in downstream markets, need to incur specific capital investment or loss in current output in order to switch to alternative inputs, the location of customers, specific investment in production process, learning and human capital in-vestment, re-tooling costs or other investments, uncertainty about quality and reputation of unknown suppliers, and others.

43. *Different categories of customers and price discrimination.* The extent of the product market might be narrowed in the presence of distinct groups of customers. A distinct group of customers for the relevant product may constitute a narrower, distinct market when such group could be subject to price discrimination. This will usually be the case when two conditions are met: a) it is possible to identify clearly which group an individual customer belongs to at

the moment of selling the relevant products to him, and b) trade among customers or arbitrage by third parties should not be feasible.

Evidence to define markets - Geographic dimension

44. The type of evidence the Commission considers relevant to reach a conclusion as to the geographic market can be categorised as follows:

45. *Past evidence of diversion of orders to other areas.* In certain cases, evidence on changes in prices between different areas and consequent reactions by customers might be available. Generally, the same quantitative tests used for product market definition might as well be used in geographic market definition, bearing in mind that international comparisons of prices might be more complex due to a number of factors such as exchange rate movements, taxation and product differentiation.

46. *Basic demand characteristics.* The nature of demand for the relevant product may in itself determine the scope of the geographical market. Factors such as national preferences or preferences for national brands, language, culture and life style, and the need for a local presence have a strong potential to limit the geographic scope of competition.

47. *Views of customers and competitors.* Where appropriate, the Commission will contact the main customers and competitors of the parties in its enquiries, to gather their views on the boundaries of the geographic market as well as most of the factual information it requires to reach a conclusion on the scope of the market when they are sufficiently backed by factual evidence.

48. *Current geographic pattern of purchases.* An examination of the customers' current geographic pattern of purchases provides useful evidence as to the possible scope of the geographic market. When customers purchase from companies located anywhere in the EU or the EEA on similar terms, or they procure their supplies through effective tendering procedures in which companies from anywhere

in the EU or the EEA do submit bids, the geographic market will be usually considered to be Community-wide.

49. *Trade flows/pattern of shipments.* When the number of customers is so large that it is not possible to obtain through them a clear picture of geographic purchasing patterns, information on trade flows might be used alternatively, provided that the trade statistics are available with a sufficient degree of detail for the relevant products. Trade flows, and above all, the rational behind trade flows provide useful insights and information for the purpose of establishing the scope of the geographic market but are not in themselves conclusive.

50. *Barriers and switching costs associated to divert orders to companies located in other areas.* The absence of transborder purchases or trade flows, for instance, does not necessarily mean that the market is at most national in scope. Still, barriers isolating the national market have to identified before concluding that the relevant geographic market in such a case is national. Perhaps the clearest obstacle for a customer to divert its orders to other areas is the impact of transport costs and transport restrictions arising from legislation or from the nature of the relevant products. The impact of transport costs will usually limit the scope of the geographic market for bulky, low value products, bearing in mind that a transport disadvantage might also be compensated by a comparative advantage in other costs (labour costs or raw materials). Access to distribution in a given area, regulatory barriers still existing in certain sectors, quotas and custom tariffs might also constitute barriers isolating a geographic area from the competitive pressure of companies located outside that area. Significant switching costs in procuring supplies from companies located in other countries constitute additional sources of such barriers.

51. On the basis of the evidence gathered, the Commission will then define a geographic market that could range from a local dimension to a global one, and there are examples of both local and global markets in past decisions of the Commission.

52. The paragraphs above describe the different factors which might be relevant to define markets. This does not imply that in each individual case it will be necessary to obtain evidence and assess each of these factors. Often in practice the evidence provided by a subset of these factors will be sufficient to reach a conclusion, as shown in the past decisional practice of the Commission.

IV. Calculation of market shares

53. The definition of the relevant market in both its product and geographic dimensions allows to identify the suppliers and the customers/consumers active on that market. On that basis, a total market size and market shares for each supplier can be calculated on the basis of their sales of the relevant products on the relevant area. In practice, the total market size and market shares are often available from market sources, i.e. companies' estimates, studies commissioned to industry consultants and/or trade associations. When this is not the case, or also when available estimates are not reliable, the Commission will usually ask each supplier in the relevant market to provide its own sales in order to calculate total market size and market shares.

54. If sales are usually the reference to calculate market shares, there are nevertheless other indications that, depending on the specific products or industry in question, can offer useful information such as, in particular, capacity, the number of players in bidding markets, units of fleet as in aerospace, or the reserves held in the case of sectors such as mining.

55. As a rule of thumb, both volume sales and value sales provide useful information. In cases of differentiated products, sales in value and their associated market share will usually be considered to better reflect the relative position and strength of each supplier.

V. Additional considerations

56. There are certain areas where the application of the principles above has to be undertaken with care. This is the case when considering primary and secondary markets, in particular, when the be-

haviour of undertakings at a point in time has to be analysed under Article 86. The method to define markets in these cases is the same, i.e. to assess the responses of customers based on their purchasing decisions to relative price changes, but taking into account as well constraints on substitution imposed by conditions in the connected markets. A narrow definition of market for secondary products, for instance, spare parts, may result when compatibility with the primary product is important. Problems of finding compatible secondary products together with the existence of high prices and a long life time of the primary products may render relative price increases of secondary products profitable. A different market definition may result if significant substitution between secondary products is possible or if the characteristics of the primary products make quick and direct consumer responses to relative price increases of the secondary products feasible.

57. In certain cases, the existence of chains of substitution might lead to the definition of a relevant market where products or areas at the extreme of the market are not directly substitutable. An example might be provided by the geographic dimension of a product with significant transport costs. In such cases, deliveries from a given plant are limited to a certain area around each plant by the impact of transport costs. In principle, such area could constitute the relevant geographic market. However, if the distribution of plants is such that there are considerable overlaps between the areas around different plants, it is possible that the pricing of those products will be constrained by a chain substitution effect, and lead to define a broader geographic market. The same reasoning may apply if product B is a demand substitute for products A and C. Even if products A and C are not direct demand substitutes they might be found to be in the same relevant product market since their respective pricing might be constrained by substitution to B.

58. From a practical perspective, the concept of chains of substitution has to be corroborated by actual evidence, for instance related to price interdependence at the extremes of the chains of substitu-

tion, in order to lead to an extension of the relevant market in an individual case. Price levels at the extremes of the chains would have to be as well of the same magnitude.

Appendix II: Excerpt from the Form CO relating to the Notification of a concentration pursuant to regulation (EC) No 139/2004
(Published in the Official Journal: OJ L 133 on 30/04/2004).

SECTION 6

Market definitions

The relevant product and geographic markets determine the scope within which the market power of the new entity resulting from the concentration must be assessed.

The notifying party or parties must provide the data requested having regard to the following definitions:

I. Relevant product markets

A relevant product market comprises all those products and/or services which are regarded as interchangeable or substitutable by the consumer, by reason of the products' characteristics, their prices and their intended use. A relevant product market may in some cases be composed of a number of individual products and/or services which present largely identical physical or technical characteristics and are interchangeable.

Factors relevant to the assessment of the relevant product market include the analysis of why the products or services in these markets are included and why others are excluded by using the above definition, and having regard to, for example, substitutability, conditions of competition, prices, cross-price elasticity of demand or other factors relevant for the definition of the product markets (for example, supply-side substitutability in appropriate cases).

II. Relevant geographic markets

The relevant geographic market comprises the area in which the undertakings concerned are involved in the supply and demand of relevant products or services, in which the conditions of competition are sufficiently homogeneous and which can be distinguished from neighbouring geographic areas because, in particular, conditions of competition are appreciably different in those areas.

Factors relevant to the assessment of the relevant geographic market include inter alia the nature and characteristics of the products or services concerned, the existence of entry barriers, consumer preferences, appreciable differences in the undertakings' market shares between neighbouring geographic areas or substantial price differences.

III. Affected markets

For purposes of information required in this Form, affected markets consist of relevant product markets where, in the EEA territory, in the Community, in the territory of the EFTA States, in any Member State or in any EFTA State:

1.) two or more of the parties to the concentration are engaged in business activities in the same product market and where the concentration will lead to a combined market share of 15 % or more. These are horizontal relationships;

2.) one or more of the parties to the concentration are engaged in business activities in a product market, which is upstream or downstream of a product market in which any other party to the concentration is engaged, and any of their individual or combined market shares at either level is 25 % or more, regardless of whether there is or is not any existing supplier/customer relationship between the parties to the concentration. These are vertical relationships.

On the basis of the above definitions and market share thresholds, provide the following information:

- Identify each affected market within the meaning of Section III, at:
- the EEA, Community or EFTA level;
- the individual Member States or EFTA States level.

In addition, state and explain the parties' view regarding the scope of the relevant geographic market within the meaning of Section II that applies in relation to each affected market identified above.

IV. Other markets in which the notified operation may have a significant impact

On the basis of the above definitions, describe the product and geographic scope of markets other than affected markets identified in Section 6.1 in which the notified operation may have a significant impact, for example, where:

1.) any of the parties to the concentration has a market share larger than 25 % and any other party to the concentration is a potential competitor into that market. A party may be considered a potential competitor, in particular, where it has plans to enter a market, or has developed or pursued such plans in the past two years;

2.) any of the parties to the concentration has a market share larger than 25 % and any other party to the concentration holds important intellectual property rights for that market;

3.) any of the parties to the concentration is present in a product market, which is a neighbouring market closely related to a product market in which any other party to the concentration is engaged, and the individual or combined market shares of the parties in any one of these markets is 25 % or more. Product markets are closely related neighbouring markets when the products are complementary to each other(18) or when they belong to a range of products that is generally purchased by the same set of customers for the same end use(19); where such markets include the whole or a part of the EEA.

In order to enable the Commission to consider, from the outset, the competitive impact of the proposed concentration in the markets identified under this Section 6.3, notifying parties are invited to submit the information under Sections 7 and 8 of this Form in relation to those markets.

Appendix III: Guidelines to the assessment of horizontal mergers under Council Regulation on the control of concentrations be-tween undertakings

(Published in the Official Journal: OJ C 31 on 5/2/2004)

I. Introduction

1. Article 2 of Council Regulation (EC) No 139/2004 of 20 January 2004 on the control of concentrations between undertakings[1] (hereinafter: the 'Merger Regulation') provides that the Commission has to appraise concentrations within the scope of the Merger Regulation with a view to establishing whether or not they are compatible with the common market. For that purpose, the Commission must assess, pursuant to Article 2(2) and (3), whether or not a concentration would significantly impede effective competition, in particular as a result of the creation or strengthening of a dominant position, in the common market or a substantial part of it.

2. Accordingly, the Commission must take into account any significant impediment to effective competition likely to be caused by a concentration. The creation or the strengthening of a dominant position is a primary form of such competitive harm. The concept of dominance was defined in the context of Council Regulation (EEC) No 4064/89 of 21 December 1989 on the control of concentrations between undertakings (hereinafter 'Regulation No 4064/89') as: 'a situation where one or more undertakings wield economic power which would enable them to prevent effective competition from being maintained in the relevant market by giving them the opportunity to act to a considerable extent independently of their competitors, their customers and, ultimately, of consumers'[2].

---

[1]   Council Regulation (EC) No 139/2004 of 20 January 2004 (OJ L 24, 29.1.2004, p. 1).
[2]   Case T-102/96, Gencor v Commission, [1999] ECR II-753, paragraph 200. See Joined Cases C-68/94 and C-30/95, France and others v Commission (hereinafter 'Kali and Salz'), [1998] ECR I-1375, paragraph 221. In exceptional circumstances, a merger may give rise to the creation or the strengthening of a dominant position on

3. For the purpose of interpreting the concept of dominance in the context of Regulation No 4064/89, the Court of Justice referred to the fact that it 'is intended to apply to all concentrations with a Community dimension insofar as they are likely, because of their effect on the structure of competition within the Community, to prove incompatible with the system of undistorted competition envisaged by the Treaty'[3].

4. The creation or strengthening of a dominant position held by a single firm as a result of a merger has been the most common basis for finding that a concentration would result in a significant impediment to effective competition. Furthermore, the concept of dominance has also been applied in an oligopolistic setting to cases of collective dominance. As a consequence, it is expected that most cases of incompatibility of a concentration with the common market will continue to be based upon a finding of dominance. That concept therefore provides an important indication as to the standard of competitive harm that is applicable when determining whether a concentration is likely to impede effective competition to a significant degree, and hence, as to the likelihood of intervention[4]. To that effect, the present notice is intended to preserve the guidance that can be drawn from past decisional practice and to take full account of past case-law of the Community Courts.

5. The purpose of this notice is to provide guidance as to how the Commission assesses concentrations[5] when the undertakings con-

---

the part of an undertaking which is not a party to the notified transaction (see Case IV/M.1383 — Exxon/Mobil, points 225-229; Case COMP/M.2434 — Grupo Villar MIR/EnBW/Hidroelectrica del Cantabrico, points 67-71).

[3] See also Joined Cases C-68/94 and C-30/95, Kali and Salz, paragraph 170.

[4] See Recitals 25 and 26 of the Merger Regulation.

[5] The term 'concentration' used in the Merger Regulation covers various types of transactions such as mergers, acquisitions, takeovers, and certain types of joint ventures. In the remainder of this notice, unless otherwise specified, the term 'merger' will be used as a synonym for concentration and therefore cover all the above types of transactions.

cerned are actual or potential competitors on the same relevant market[6]. In this notice such mergers will be denoted 'horizontal mergers'. While the notice presents the analytical approach used by the Commission in its appraisal of horizontal mergers it cannot provide details of all possible applications of this approach. The Commission applies the approach described in the notice to the particular facts and circumstances of each case.

6. The guidance set out in this notice draws and elaborates on the Commission's evolving experience with the appraisal of horizontal mergers under Regulation No 4064/89 since its entry into force on September 1990 as well as on the case-law of the Court of Justice and the Court of First Instance of the European Communities. The principles contained here will be applied and further developed and refined by the Commission in individual cases. The Commission may revise this notice from time to time in the light of future developments.

7. The Commission's interpretation of the Merger Regulation as regards the appraisal of horizontal mergers is without prejudice to the interpretation which may be given by the Court of Justice or the Court of First Instance of the European Communities.

II. Overview

8. Effective competition brings benefits to consumers, such as low prices, high quality products, a wide selection of goods and services, and innovation. Through its control of mergers, the Commission prevents mergers that would be likely to deprive customers of these benefits by significantly increasing the market power of firms. By 'increased market power' is meant the ability of one or more firms to profitably increase prices, reduce output, choice or quality

---

[6] The notice does not cover the assessment of the effects of competition that a merger has in other markets, including vertical and conglomerate effects. Nor does it cover the assessment of the effects of a joint venture as referred to in Article 2(4) of the Merger Regulation.

of goods and services, diminish innovation, or otherwise influence parameters of competition. In this notice, the expression 'increased prices' is often used as shorthand for these various ways in which a merger may result in competitive harm[7]. Both suppliers and buyers can have market power. However, for clarity, market power will usually refer here to a supplier's market power. Where a buyer's market power is the issue, the term 'buyer power' is employed.

9. In assessing the competitive effects of a merger, the Commission compares the competitive conditions that would result from the notified merger with the conditions that would have prevailed without the merger[8]. In most cases the competitive conditions existing at the time of the merger constitute the relevant comparison for evaluating the effects of a merger. However, in some circumstances, the Commission may take into account future changes to the market that can reasonably be predicted[9]. It may, in particular, take account of the likely entry or exit of firms if the merger did not take place when considering what constitutes the relevant comparison[10].

10. The Commission's assessment of mergers normally entails:

(a) definition of the relevant product and geographic markets;

(b) competitive assessment of the merger.

---

[7]   The expression should be understood to also cover situations where, for instance, prices are decreased less, or are less likely to decrease, than they otherwise would have without the merger and where prices are increased more, or are more likely to increase, than they otherwise would have without the merger.

[8]   By analogy, in the case of a merger that has been implemented without having been notified, the Commission would assess the merger in the light of the competitive conditions that would have prevailed without the implemented merger.

[9]   See, e.g. Commission Decision 98/526/EC in Case IV/M.950 — Hoffmann La Roche/Boehringer Mannheim, OJ L 234, 21.8.1998, p. 14, point 13; Case IV/M.1846 — Glaxo Wellcome/SmithKline Beecham, points 70-72; Case COMP/M.2547 — Bayer/Aventis Crop Science, points 324 et seq.

[10]   See, e.g. Case T-102/96, Gencor v Commission, [1999] ECR II-753, paragraphs 247-263.

The main purpose of market definition is to identify in a systematic way the immediate competitive constraints facing the merged entity. Guidance on this issue can be found in the Commission's Notice on the definition of the relevant market for the purposes of Community competition law [11]. Various considerations leading to the delineation of the relevant markets may also be of importance for the competitive assessment of the merger.

11. This notice is structured around the following elements:

(a) The approach of the Commission to market shares and concentration thresholds (Section III).

(b) The likelihood that a merger would have anticompetitive effects in the relevant markets, in the absence of countervailing factors (Section IV).

(c) The likelihood that buyer power would act as a countervailing factor to an increase in market power resulting from the merger (Section V).

(d) The likelihood that entry would maintain effective competition in the relevant markets (Section VI).

(e) The likelihood that efficiencies would act as a factor counteracting the harmful effects on competition which might otherwise result from the merger (Section VII).

(f) The conditions for a failing firm defence (Section VIII).

12. In order to assess the foreseeable impact[12] of a merger on the relevant markets, the Commission analyses its possible anticompetitive effects and the relevant countervailing factors such as buyer power, the extent of entry barriers and possible efficiencies put forward by the parties. In exceptional circumstances, the Com-

---

[11] OJ C 372, 9.12.1997, p. 5.
[12] See Case T-102/96, Gencor v Commission, [1999] ECR II-753, paragraph 262, and Case T-342/99, Airtours v Commission, [2002] ECR II-2585, paragraph 280.

mission considers whether the conditions for a failing firm defence are met.

13. In the light of these elements, the Commission determines, pursuant to Article 2 of the Merger Regulation, whether the merger would significantly impede effective competition, in particular through the creation or the strengthening of a dominant position, and should therefore be declared incompatible with the common market. It should be stressed that these factors are not a 'checklist' to be mechanically applied in each and every case. Rather, the competitive analysis in a particular case will be based on an overall assessment of the foreseeable impact of the merger in the light of the relevant factors and conditions. Not all the elements will always be relevant to each and every horizontal merger, and it may not be necessary to analyse all the elements of a case in the same detail.

III. Market share and concentration levels

14. Market shares and concentration levels provide useful first indications of the market structure and of the competitive importance of both the merging parties and their competitors.

15. Normally, the Commission uses current market shares in its competitive analysis[13]. However, current market shares may be adjusted to reflect reasonably certain future changes, for instance in the light of exit, entry or expansion[14]. Post-merger market shares are calculated on the assumption that the post-merger combined market share of the merging parties is the sum of their pre-merger market shares[15]. Historic data may be used if market shares have been

---

[13]   As to the calculation of market shares, see also Commission Notice on the definition of the relevant market for the purposes of Community competition law, OJ C 372, 9.12.1997, p. 3, paragraphs 54-55.

[14]   See, e.g. Case COMP/M.1806 — Astra Zeneca/Novartis, points 150 and 415.

[15]   When relevant, market shares may be adjusted, in particular, to account for controlling interests in other firms (See, e.g. Case IV/M.1383 — Exxon/Mobil, points 446-458; Case COMP/M.1879 — Boeing/Hughes, points 60-79; Case COMP/JV 55 — Hutchison/RCPM/ECT, points 66-75), or for other arrangements with third parties

volatile, for instance when the market is characterised by large, lumpy orders. Changes in historic market shares may provide useful information about the competitive process and the likely future importance of the various competitors, for instance, by indicating whether firms have been gaining or losing market shares. In any event, the Commission interprets market shares in the light of likely market conditions, for instance, if the market is highly dynamic in character and if the market structure is unstable due to innovation or growth[16].

16. The overall concentration level in a market may also provide useful information about the competitive situation. In order to measure concentration levels, the Commission often applies the Herfindahl-Hirschman Index (HHI)[17]. The HHI is calculated by summing the squares of the individual market shares of all the firms in the market[18]. The HHI gives proportionately greater weight to the market shares of the larger firms. Although it is best to include all firms in the calculation, lack of information about very small firms may not be important because such firms do not affect the HHI significantly. While the absolute level of the HHI can give an initial indication of the competitive pressure in the market post-merger, the change in the HHI (known as the 'delta') is a useful

---

(See, for instance, as regards sub-contractors, Commission Decision 2001/769/EC in Case COMP/M.1940 — Framatome/Siemens/Cogema, OJ L 289, 6.11.2001, p. 8, point 142).

[16] See, e.g. Case COMP/M.2256 — Philips/Agilent Health Care Technologies, points 31-32, and Case COMP/M.2609 — HP/Compaq, point 39.

[17] See, e.g. Case IV/M.1365 — FCC/Vivendi, point 40; Case COMP/JV 55 — Hutchison/RCPM/ECT, point 50. If appropriate, the Commission may also use other concentration measures such as, for instance, concentration ratios, which measure the aggregate market share of a small number (usually three or four) of the leading firms in a market

[18] For example, a market containing five firms with market shares of 40 %, 20 %, 15 %, 15 %, and 10 %, respectively, has an HHI of 2 550 ($40^2 + 20^2 + 15^2 + 15^2 + 10^2 =$ 2 550). The HHI ranges from close to zero (in an atomistic market) to 10 000 (in the case of a pure monopoly).

proxy for the change in concentration directly brought about by the merger[19].

Market share levels

17. According to well-established case law, very large market shares — 50 % or more — may in themselves be evidence of the existence of a dominant market position[20]. However, smaller competitors may act as a sufficient constraining influence if, for example, they have the ability and incentive to increase their supplies. A merger involving a firm whose market share will remain below 50 % after the merger may also raise competition concerns in view of other factors such as the strength and number of competitors, the presence of capacity constraints or the extent to which the products of the merging parties are close substitutes. The Commission has thus in several cases considered mergers resulting in firms holding market shares between 40 % and 50 %[21], and in some cases below 40 %[22], to lead to the creation or the strengthening of a dominant position.

18. Concentrations which, by reason of the limited market share of the undertakings concerned, are not liable to impede effective competition may be presumed to be compatible with the common mar-

---

[19] The increase in concentration as measured by the HHI can be calculated independently of the overall market concentration by doubling the product of the market shares of the merging firms. For example, a merger of two firms with market shares of 30 % and 15 % respectively would increase the HHI by 900 (30 × 15 × 2 = 900). The explanation for this technique is as follows: Before the merger, the market shares of the merging firms contribute to the HHI by their squares individually: (a)2 + (b)2. After the merger, the contribution is the square of their sum: (a + b)2, which equals (a)2 + (b)2 + 2ab. The increase in the HHI is therefore represented by 2ab.

[20] Case T-221/95, Endemol v Commission, [1999] ECR II-1299, paragraph 134, and Case T-102/96, Gencor v Commission, [1999] ECR II-753, paragraph 205. It is a distinct question whether a dominant position is created or strengthened as a result of the merger.

[21] See, e.g. Case COMP/M.2337 — Nestlé/Ralston Purina, points 48-50.

[22] See, e.g. Commission Decision 1999/674/EC in Case IV/M.1221 — Rewe/Meinl, OJ L 274, 23.10.1999, p. 1, points 98-114; Case COMP/M.2337 — Nestlé/Ralston Purina, points 44-47.

ket. Without prejudice to Articles 81 and 82 of the Treaty, an indication to this effect exists, in particular, where the market share of the undertakings concerned does not exceed 25 %[23] either in the common market or in a substantial part of it[24].

HHI levels

19. The Commission is unlikely to identify horizontal competition concerns in a market with a post-merger HHI below 1 000. Such markets normally do not require extensive analysis.

20. The Commission is also unlikely to identify horizontal competition concerns in a merger with a post-merger HHI between 1 000 and 2 000 and a delta below 250, or a merger with a post-merger HHI above 2 000 and a delta below 150, except where special circumstances such as, for instance, one or more of the following factors are present:

(a) a merger involves a potential entrant or a recent entrant with a small market share;

(b) one or more merging parties are important innovators in ways not reflected in market shares;

(c) there are significant cross-shareholdings among the market participants[25];

---

[23] The calculation of market shares depends critically on market definition. It must be emphasised that the Commission does not necessarily accept the parties' proposed market definition.

[24] Recital 32 of the Merger Regulation. However, such an indication does not apply to cases where the proposed merger creates or strengthens a collective dominant position involving the 'undertakings concerned' and other third parties (see Joined Cases C-68/94 and C-30/95, Kali and Salz, [1998] ECR I-1375, paragraphs 171 et seq.; and Case T-102/96, Gencor v Commission, [1999] ECR II-753, paragraphs 134 et seq.).

[25] In markets with cross-shareholdings or joint ventures the Commission may use a modified HHI, which takes into account such share-holdings (see, e.g. Case IV/M.1383 — Exxon/Mobil, point 256). 5.2.2004 EN Official Journal of the European Union C 31/15

(d) one of the merging firms is a maverick firm with a high likelihood of disrupting coordinated conduct;

(e) indications of past or ongoing coordination, or facilitating practices, are present;

(f) one of the merging parties has a pre-merger market share of 50 % of more[26].

21. Each of these HHI levels, in combination with the relevant deltas, may be used as an initial indicator of the absence of competition concerns. However, they do not give rise to a presumption of either the existence or the absence of such concerns.

IV. Possible anti-competitive effects of horizontal mergers

22. There are two main ways in which horizontal mergers may significantly impede effective competition, in particular by creating or strengthening a dominant position:

(a) by eliminating important competitive constraints on one or more firms, which consequently would have increased market power, without resorting to coordinated behaviour (non-coordinated effects);

(b) by changing the nature of competition in such a way that firms that previously were not coordinating their behaviour, are now significantly more likely to coordinate and raise prices or otherwise harm effective competition. A merger may also make coordination easier, more stable or more effective for firms which were coordinating prior to the merger (coordinated effects).

23. The Commission assesses whether the changes brought about by the merger would result in any of these effects. Both instances mentioned above may be relevant when assessing a particular transaction.

---

[26] See paragraph 17.

Non-coordinated effects[27]

24. A merger may significantly impede effective competition in a market by removing important competitive constraints on one or more sellers, who consequently have increased market power. The most direct effect of the merger will be the loss of competition between the merging firms. For example, if prior to the merger one of the merging firms had raised its price, it would have lost some sales to the other merging firm. The merger removes this particular constraint. Non-merging firms in the same market can also benefit from the reduction of competitive pressure that results from the merger, since the merging firms' price increase may switch some demand to the rival firms, which, in turn, may find it profitable to increase their prices[28]. The reduction in these competitive constraints could lead to significant price increases in the relevant market.

25. Generally, a merger giving rise to such non-coordinated effects would significantly impede effective competition by creating or strengthening the dominant position of a single firm, one which, typically, would have an appreciably larger market share than the next competitor post-merger. Furthermore, mergers in oligopolistic markets[29] involving the elimination of important competitive constraints that the merging parties previously exerted upon each other together with a reduction of competitive pressure on the remaining competitors may, even where there is little likelihood of coordination between the members of the oligopoly, also result in a significant impediment to competition. The Merger Regulation clarifies

---

[27] Also often called 'unilateral' effects.
[28] Such expected reactions by competitors may be a relevant factor influencing the merged entity's incentives to increase prices.
[29] An oligopolistic market refers to a market structure with a limited number of sizeable firms. Because the behaviour of one firm has anappreciable impact on the overall market conditions, and thus indirectly on the situation of each of the other firms, oligopolistic firms are interdependent.

that all mergers giving rise to such non-coordinated effects shall also be declared incompatible with the common market[30].

26. A number of factors, which taken separately are not necessarily decisive, may influence whether significant non-coordinated effects are likely to result from a merger. Not all of these factors need to be present for such effects to be likely. Nor should this be considered an exhaustive list.

Merging firms have large market shares

27. The larger the market share, the more likely a firm is to possess market power. And the larger the addition of market share, the more likely it is that a merger will lead to a significant increase in market power. The larger the increase in the sales base on which to enjoy higher margins after a price increase, the more likely it is that the merging firms will find such a price increase profitable despite the accompanying reduction in output. Although market shares and additions of market shares only provide first indications of market power and increases in market power, they are normally important factors in the assessment[31].

Merging firms are close competitors

28. Products may be differentiated[32] within a relevant market such that some products are closer substitutes than others[33]. The higher

---

[30] Recital 25 of the Merger Regulation.

[31] See, in particular, paragraphs 17 and 18.

[32] Products may be differentiated in various ways. There may, for example, be differentiation in terms of geographic location, based on branch or stores location; location matters for retail distribution, banks, travel agencies, or petrol stations. Likewise, differentiation may be based on brand image, technical specifications, quality or level of service. The level of advertising in a market may be an indicator of the firms' effort to differentiate their products. For other products, buyers may have to incur switching costs to use a competitor's product.

[33] For the definition of the relevant market, see the Commission's Notice on the definition of the relevant market for the purposes of Community competition law, cited above.

the degree of substitutability between the merging firms' products, the more likely it is that the merging firms will raise prices significantly[34]. For example, a merger between two producers offering products which a substantial number of customers regard as their first and second choices could generate a significant price increase. Thus, the fact that rivalry between the parties has been an important source of competition on the market may be a central factor in the analysis[35]. High pre-merger margins[36] may also make significant price increases more likely. The merging firms' incentive to raise prices is more likely to be constrained when rival firms produce close substitutes to the products of the merging firms than when they offer less close substitutes[37]. It is therefore less likely that a merger will significantly impede effective competition, in particular through the creation or strengthening of a dominant position, when there is a high degree of substitutability between the products of the merging firms and those supplied by rival producers.

29. When data are available, the degree of substitutability may be evaluated through customer preference surveys, analysis of purchasing patterns, estimation of the cross-price elasticities of the

---

[34] See for example Case COMP/M.2817 – Barilla/BPS/Kamps, point 34; Commission Decision 2001/403/EC in Case COMP/M.1672 – Volvo/ Scania, OJ L 143, 29.5.2001, p. 74, points 107-148.

[35] See, e.g. Commission Decision 94/893/EC in Case IV/M.430 – Procter & Gamble/VP Schickedanz (II), OJ L 354, 21.6.1994, p. 32, Case T-290/94, Kaysersberg v Commission, [1997] II-2137, paragraph 153; Commission Decision 97/610/EC in Case IV/M.774 – Saint-Gobain/ Wacker-Chemie/NOM, OJ L 247, 10.9.1997, p. 1, point 179; Commission Decision 2002/156/EC in Case COMP/M.2097 – SCA/Metsä Tissue, OJ L 57, 27.2.2002, p. 1, points 94-108; Case T-310/01, Schneider v Commission, [2002] II-4071, paragraph 418.

[36] Typically, the relevant margin (m) is the difference between price (p) and the incremental cost (c) of supplying one more unit of output expressed as a percentage of price ($m = (p - c)p)$).

[37] See, e.g. Case IV/M.1980 – Volvo/Renault VI, point 34; Case COMP/M.2256 – Philips Agilent/Health Care Solutions, points 33-35; Case COMP/M.2537 – Philips/Marconi Medical Systems, points 31-34.

products involved[38], or diversion ratios[39]. In bidding markets it may be possible to measure whether historically the submitted bids by one of the merging parties have been constrained by the presence of the other merging party[40].

30. In some markets it may be relatively easy and not too costly for the active firms to reposition their products or extend their product portfolio. In particular, the Commission examines whether the possibility of repositioning or product line extension by competitors or the merging parties may influence the incentive of the merged entity to raise prices. However, product repositioning or product line extension often entails risks and large sunk costs[41] and may be less profitable than the current line.

Customers have limited possibilities of switching supplier

31. Customers of the merging parties may have difficulties switching to other suppliers[42] because there are few alternative suppliers or because they face substantial switching costs[43]. Such customers are particularly vulnerable to price increases. The merger may affect these customers' ability to protect themselves against price increases. In particular, this may be the case for customers that have

---

[38] The cross-price elasticity of demand measures the extent to which the quantity of a product demanded changes in response to a change in the price of some other product, all other things remaining equal. The own-price elasticity measures the extent to which demand for a product changes in response to the change in the price of the product itself.

[39] The diversion ratio from product A to product B measures the proportion of the sales of product A lost due to a price increase of A that are captured by product B.

[40] Commission Decision 97/816/EC in Case IV/M.877 − Boeing/McDonnell Douglas, OJ L 336, 8.12.1997, p. 16, points 58 et seq.; Case COMP/M.3083 − GE/Instrumentarium, points 125 et seq.

[41] Sunk costs are costs which are unrecoverable upon exit from the market.

[42] See e.g. Commission Decision 2002/156/EC in Case IV/M.877 − Boeing/McDonnell Douglas, OJ L 336, 8.12.1997, p. 16, point 70.

[43] See, e.g. Case IV/M. 986 − Agfa Gevaert/DuPont, OJ L 211, 29.7.1998, p. 22, points 63-71.

used dual sourcing from the two merging firms as a means of obtaining competitive prices. Evidence of past customer switching patterns and reactions to price changes may provide important information in this respect.

Competitors are unlikely to increase supply if prices increase

32. When market conditions are such that the competitors of the merging parties are unlikely to increase their supply substantially if prices increase, the merging firms may have an incentive to reduce output below the combined pre-merger levels, thereby raising market prices[44]. The merger increases the incentive to reduce output by giving the merged firm a larger base of sales on which to enjoy the higher margins resulting from an increase in prices induced by the output reduction.

33. Conversely, when market conditions are such that rival firms have enough capacity and find it profitable to expand output sufficiently, the Commission is unlikely to find that the merger will create or strengthen a dominant position or otherwise significantly impede effective competition.

34. Such output expansion is, in particular, unlikely when competitors face binding capacity constraints and the expansion of capacity is costly[45] or if existing excess capacity is significantly more costly to operate than capacity currently in use.

35. Although capacity constraints are more likely to be important when goods are relatively homogeneous, they may also be important where firms offer differentiated products.

---

[44] See, e.g. Case COMP/M.2187 – CVC/Lenzing, points 162-170.
[45] When analysing the possible expansion of capacity by rivals, the Commission considers factors similar to those described in Section VI on entry.See, e.g. Case COMP/M.2187 – CVC/Lenzing, points 162-173.

Merged entity able to hinder expansion by competitors
36. Some proposed mergers would, if allowed to proceed, significantly impede effective competition by leaving the merged firm in a position where it would have the ability and incentive to make the expansion of smaller firms and potential competitors more difficult or otherwise restrict the ability of rival firms to compete. In such a case, competitors may not, either individually or in the aggregate, be in a position to constrain the merged entity to such a degree that it would not increase prices or take other actions detrimental to competition. For instance, the merged entity may have such a degree of control, or influence over, the supply of inputs[46] or distribution possibilities[47] that expansion or entry by rival firms may be more costly. Similarly, the merged entity's control over patents[48] or other types of intellectual property (e.g. brands[49]) may make expansion or entry by rivals more difficult. In markets where interoperability between different infrastructures or platforms is important[50], a merger may give the merged entity the ability and incentive to raise the costs or decrease the quality of service of its rivals[51]. In making

---

[46] See, e.g. Case T-221/95, Endemol v Commission, [1999] ECR II-1299, paragraph 167.
[47] See, e.g. Case T-22/97, Kesko v Commission, [1999], ECR II-3775, paragraphs 141 et seq.
[48] See, e.g. Commission Decision 2001/684/EC in Case M.1671 – Dow Chemical/Union Carbide OJ L 245, 4.9.2001, p. 1, points 107-114.
[49] See, e.g. Commission Decision 96/435/EC in Case IV/M.623 – Kimberly-Clark/Scott, OJ L 183, 23.7.1996, p. 1; Case T-114/02, Babyliss SA v Commission ('Seb/Moulinex'), [2003] ECR II-000, paragraphs 343 et seq.
[50] This is, for example, the case in network industries such as energy, telecommunications and other communication industries.
[51] Commission Decision 99/287/EC in Case IV/M.1069 – Worldcom/MCI, OJ L 116, 4.5.1999, p. 1, points 117 et seq.; Case IV/M.1741 – MCI Worldcom/Sprint, points 145 et seq.; Case IV/M.1795 – Vodafone Airtouch/Mannesmann, points 44 et seq.

this assessment the Commission may take into account, inter alia, the financial strength of the merged entity relative to its rivals[52].

Merger eliminates an important competitive force

37. Some firms have more of an influence on the competitive process than their market shares or similar measures would suggest. A merger involving such a firm may change the competitive dynamics in a significant, anticompetitive way, in particular when the market is already concentrated[53]. For instance, a firm may be a recent entrant that is expected to exert significant competitive pressure in the future on the other firms in the market.

38. In markets where innovation is an important competitive force, a merger may increase the firms' ability and incentive to bring new innovations to the market and, thereby, the competitive pressure on rivals to innovate in that market. Alternatively, effective competition may be significantly impeded by a merger between two important innovators, for instance between two companies with 'pipeline' products related to a specific product market. Similarly, a firm with a relatively small market share may nevertheless be an important competitive force if it has promising pipeline products[54].

Coordinated effects

39. In some markets the structure may be such that firms would consider it possible, economically rational, and hence preferable, to adopt on a sustainable basis a course of action on the market aimed at selling at increased prices. A merger in a concentrated market may significantly impede effective competition, through the crea-

---

[52] Case T-156/98 RJB Mining v Commission [2001] ECR II-337.
[53] Commission Decision 2002/156/EC in Case IV/M.877 − Boeing/McDonnell Douglas, OJ L 336, 8.12.1997, p. 16, point 58; Case COMP/M.2568 − Haniel/Ytong, point 126.
[54] For an example of pipeline products of one merging party likely to compete with the other party's pipeline or existing products, see, e.g. Case IV/M.1846 − Glaxo Wellcome/SmithKline Beecham, point 188.

tion or the strengthening of a collective dominant position, because it increases the likelihood that firms are able to coordinate their behaviour in this way and raise prices, even without entering into an agreement or resorting to a concerted practice within the meaning of Article 81 of the Treaty[55]. A merger may also make coordination easier, more stable or more effective for firms, that were already coordinating before the merger, either by making the coordination more robust or by permitting firms to coordinate on even higher prices.

40. Coordination may take various forms. In some markets, the most likely coordination may involve keeping prices above the competitive level. In other markets, coordination may aim at limiting production or the amount of new capacity brought to the market. Firms may also coordinate by dividing the market, for instance by geo-graphic area[56] or other customer characteristics, or by allocating contracts in bidding markets.

41. Coordination is more likely to emerge in markets where it is relatively simple to reach a common understanding on the terms of co-ordination. In addition, three conditions are necessary for coordination to be sustainable. First, the coordinating firms must be able to monitor to a sufficient degree whether the terms of coordination are being adhered to. Second, discipline requires that there is some form of credible deterrent mechanism that can be activated if deviation is detected. Third, the reactions of outsiders, such as current and future competitors not participating in the coordination, as well as customers, should not be able to jeopardise the results expected from the coordination[57].

---

[55] Case T-102/96, Gencor v Commission, [1999] ECR II-753, paragraph 277; Case T-342/99, Airtours v Commission, [2002] ECR II-2585, paragraph 61.
[56] This may be the case if the oligopolists have tended to concentrate their sales in different areas for historic reasons. C 31/16 EN Official Journal of the European Union 5.2.2004
[57] Case T-342/99, Airtours v Commission, [2002] ECR II-2585, paragraph 62.

42. The Commission examines whether it would be possible to reach terms of coordination and whether the coordination is likely to be sustainable. In this respect, the Commission considers the changes that the merger brings about. The reduction in the number of firms in a market may, in itself, be a factor that facilitates coordination. However, a merger may also increase the likelihood or significance of coordinated effects in other ways. For instance, a merger may involve a 'maverick' firm that has a history of preventing or disrupting coordination, for example by failing to follow price increases by its competitors, or has characteristics that gives it an incentive to favour different strategic choices than its coordinating competitors would prefer. If the merged firm were to adopt strategies similar to those of other competitors, the remaining firms would find it easier to coordinate, and the merger would increase the likelihood, stability or effectiveness of coordination.

43. In assessing the likelihood of coordinated effects, the Commission takes into account all available relevant information on the characteristics of the markets concerned, including both structural features and the past behaviour of firms[58]. Evidence of past coordination is important if the relevant market characteristics have not changed appreciably or are not likely to do so in the near future[59]. Likewise, evidence of coordination in similar markets may be useful information.

Reaching terms of coordination

44. Coordination is more likely to emerge if competitors can easily arrive at a common perception as to how the coordination should work. Coordinating firms should have similar views regarding which actions would be considered to be in accordance with the aligned behaviour and which actions would not.

---

[58] See Commission Decision 92/553/EC in Case IV/M.190 — Nestlé/Perrier, OJ L 356, 5.12.1992, p. 1, points 117-118.
[59] See, e.g. Case IV/M.580 — ABB/Daimler-Benz, point 95.

45. Generally, the less complex and the more stable the economic environment, the easier it is for the firms to reach a common understanding on the terms of coordination. For instance, it is easier to coordinate among a few players than among many. It is also easier to coordinate on a price for a single, homogeneous product, than on hundreds of prices in a market with many differentiated products. Similarly, it is easier to coordinate on a price when demand and supply conditions are relatively stable than when they are continuously changing[60]. In this context volatile demand, substantial internal growth by some firms in the market or frequent entry by new firms may indicate that the current situation is not sufficiently stable to make coordination likely[61]. In markets where innovation is important, coordination may be more difficult since innovations, particularly significant ones, may allow one firm to gain a major advantage over its rivals.

46. Coordination by way of market division will be easier if customers have simple characteristics that allow the coordinating firms to readily allocate them. Such characteristics may be based on geography; on customer type or simply on the existence of customers who typically buy from one specific firm. Coordination by way of market division may be relatively straightforward if it is easy to identify each customer's supplier and the coordination device is the allocation of existing customers to their incumbent supplier.

47. Coordinating firms may, however, find other ways to overcome problems stemming from complex economic environments short of market division. They may, for instance, establish simple pricing rules that reduce the complexity of coordinating on a large number of prices. One example of such a rule is establishing a small number of pricing points, thus reducing the coordination problem. Another

---

[60] See, e.g. Commission Decision 2002/156/EC in Case COMP/M.2097 — SCA/Metsä Tissue, OJ L 57, 27.2.2002, p. 1, point 148.
[61] See, e.g. Case IV/M.1298 — Kodak/Imation, point 60.

example is having a fixed relationship between certain base prices and a number of other prices, such that prices basically move in parallel. Publicly available key information, exchange of information through trade associations, or information received through cross-shareholdings or participation in joint ventures may also help firms reach terms of coordination. The more complex the market situation is, the more transparency or communication is likely to be needed to reach a common understanding on the terms of coordination.

48. Firms may find it easier to reach a common understanding on the terms of coordination if they are relatively symmetric[62], especially in terms of cost structures, market shares, capacity levels and levels of vertical integration[63]. Structural links such as cross-shareholding or participation in joint ventures may also help in aligning incentives among the coordinating firms[64].

Monitoring deviations

49. Coordinating firms are often tempted to increase their share of the market by deviating from the terms of coordination, for instance by lowering prices, offering secret discounts, increasing product quality or capacity or trying to win new customers. Only the credible threat of timely and sufficient retaliation keeps firms from deviating. Markets therefore need to be sufficiently transparent to allow

---

[62] Case T-102/96, Gencor v Commission, [1999] ECR II-753, paragraph 222; Commission Decision 92/553/EC in Case IV/M.190 – Nestlé/Perrier,OJ L 356, 5.12.1992, p. 1, points 63-123.

[63] In assessing whether or not a merger may increase the symmetry of the various firms present on the market, efficiency gains may provide important indications (see also paragraph 82 of the notice).

[64] See, e.g. Commission Decision 2001/519/EC in Case COMP/M.1673 – VEBA/VIAG, OJ L 188, 10.7.2001, p. 1, point 226; Case COMP/M.2567 – Nordbanken/Postgirot, point 54.

the coordinating firms to monitor to a sufficient degree whether other firms are deviating, and thus know when to retaliate[65].

50. Transparency in the market is often higher, the lower the number of active participants in the market. Further, the degree of transparency often depends on how market transactions take place in a particular market. For example, transparency is likely to be high in a market where transactions take place on a public exchange or in an open outcry auction[66]. Conversely, transparency may be low in a market where transactions are confidentially negotiated between buyers and sellers on a bilateral basis[67]. When evaluating the level of transparency in the market, the key element is to identify what firms can infer about the actions of other firms from the available information[68]. Coordinating firms should be able to interpret with some certainty whether unexpected behaviour is the result of deviation from the terms of coordination. For instance, in unstable environments it may be difficult for a firm to know whether its lost sales are due to an overall low level of demand or due to a competitor offering particularly low prices. Similarly, when overall demand or cost conditions fluctuate, it may be difficult to interpret whether a competitor is lowering its price because it expects the coordinated prices to fall or because it is deviating.

51. In some markets where the general conditions may seem to make monitoring of deviations difficult, firms may nevertheless engage in practices which have the effect of easing the monitoring task, even when these practices are not necessarily entered into for such

---

[65] See, e.g. Case COMP/M.2389 – Shell/DEA, points 112 et seq.; and Case COMP/M.2533 – BP/E.ON, points 102 et seq.

[66] See also Commission Decision 2000/42/EC in Case IV/M.1313 – Danish Crown/Vestjyske Slagterier, OJ L 20, 25.1.2000, p. 1, points 176-179.

[67] See, e.g. Case COMP/M.2640 – Nestlé/Schöller, point 37; Commission Decision 1999/641/EC in Case COMP/M.1225 – Enso/Stora, OJ L 254,29.9.1999, p. 9, points 67-68.

[68] See, e.g. Case IV/M.1939 – Rexam (PLM)/American National Can, point 24.

purposes. These practices, such as meeting-competition or most-favoured customer clauses, voluntary publication of information, announcements, or exchange of information through trade associations, may increase transparency or help competitors interpret the choices made. Cross-directorships, participation in joint ventures and similar arrangements may also make monitoring easier.

Deterrent mechanisms

52. Coordination is not sustainable unless the consequences of deviation are sufficiently severe to convince coordinating firms that it is in their best interest to adhere to the terms of coordination. It is thus the threat of future retaliation that keeps the coordination sustainable[69]. However the threat is only credible if, where deviation by one of the firms is detected, there is sufficient certainty that some deterrent mechanism will be activated[70].

53. Retaliation that manifests itself after some significant time lag, or is not certain to be activated, is less likely to be sufficient to offset the benefits from deviating. For example, if a market is characterised by infrequent, large-volume orders, it may be difficult to establish a sufficiently severe deterrent mechanism, since the gain from deviating at the right time may be large, certain and immediate, whereas the losses from being punished may be small and uncertain and only materialise after some time. The speed with which deterrent mechanisms can be implemented is related to the issue of transparency. If firms are only able to observe their competitors' actions after a substantial delay, then retaliation will be similarly de-

---

[69] See Case COMP/M.2389 – Shell/DEA, point 121, and Case COMP/M.2533 – BP/E.ON, point 111.

[70] Although deterrent mechanisms are sometimes called 'punishment' mechanisms, this should not be understood in the strict sense that such a mechanism necessarily punishes individually a firm that has deviated. The expectation that coordination may break down for a certain period of time, if a deviation is identified as such, may in itself constitute a sufficient deterrent mechanism.

layed and this may influence whether it is sufficient to deter deviation.

54. The credibility of the deterrence mechanism depends on whether the other coordinating firms have an incentive to retaliate. Some deterrent mechanisms, such as punishing the deviator by temporarily engaging in a price war or increasing output significantly, may entail a short-term economic loss for the firms carrying out the retaliation. This does not necessarily remove the incentive to retaliate since the short-term loss may be smaller than the long-term benefit of retaliating resulting from the return to the regime of coordination.

55. Retaliation need not necessarily take place in the same market as the deviation[71]. If the coordinating firms have commercial interaction in other markets, these may offer various methods of retaliation[72]. The retaliation could take many forms, including cancellation of joint ventures or other forms of cooperation or selling of shares in jointly owned companies.

Reactions of outsiders

56. For coordination to be successful, the actions of non-coordinating firms and potential competitors, as well as customers, should not be able to jeopardise the outcome expected from coordination. For example, if coordination aims at reducing overall capacity in the market, this will only hurt consumers if non-coordinating firms are unable or have no incentive to respond to this decrease by increasing their own capacity sufficiently to prevent a net decrease in capacity, or at least to render the coordinated capacity decrease unprofitable[73].

---

[71] See, e.g. Commission Decision 2000/42/EC in Case IV/M.1313 – Danish Crown/Vestjyske Slagterier, OJ L 20, 25.1.2000, p. 1, point 177.
[72] See Case T-102/96, Gencor v Commission, [1999] ECR II-753, paragraph 281.
[73] These elements are analysed in a similar way to non-coordinated effects.

57. The effects of entry and countervailing buyer power of customers are analysed in later sections. However, special consideration is given to the possible impact of these elements on the stability of coordination. For instance, by concentrating a large amount of its requirements with one supplier or by offering long-term contracts, a large buyer may make coordination unstable by successfully tempting one of the coordinating firms to deviate in order to gain substantial new business.

Merger with a potential competitor

58. Concentrations where an undertaking already active on a relevant market merges with a potential competitor in this market can have similar anti-competitive effects to mergers between two undertakings already active on the same relevant market and, thus, significantly impede effective competition, in particular through the creation or the strengthening of a dominant position.

59. A merger with a potential competitor can generate horizontal anti-competitive effects, whether coordinated or non-coordinated, if the potential competitor significantly constrains the behaviour of the firms active in the market. This is the case if the potential competitor possesses assets that could easily be used to enter the market without incurring significant sunk costs. Anticompetitive effects may also occur where the merging partner is very likely to incur the necessary sunk costs to enter the market in a relatively short period of time after which this company would constrain the behaviour of the firms currently active in the market[74].

60. For a merger with a potential competitor to have significant anti-competitive effects, two basic conditions must be fulfilled. First, the potential competitor must already exert a significant constraining

---

74 See, e.g. Case IV/M.1630 – Air Liquide/BOC, points 201 et seq. For an example of a case where entry by the other merging firm was not sufficiently likely in the short to medium term (Case T-158/00, ARD v Commission, [2003] ECR II-000, paragraphs 115-127).

influence or there must be a significant likelihood that it would grow into an effective competitive force. Evidence that a potential competitor has plans to enter a market in a significant way could help the Commission to reach such a conclusion[75]. Second, there must not be a sufficient number of other potential competitors, which could maintain sufficient competitive pressure after the merger[76].

Mergers creating or strengthening buyer power in upstream markets

61. The Commission may also analyse to what extent a merged entity will increase its buyer power in upstream markets. On the one hand, a merger that creates or strengthens the market power of a buyer may significantly impede effective competition, in particular by creating or strengthening a dominant position. The merged firm may be in a position to obtain lower prices by reducing its purchase of inputs. This may, in turn, lead it also to lower its level of output in the final product market, and thus harm consumer welfare[77]. Such effects may in particular arise when upstream sellers are relatively fragmented. Competition in the downstream markets could also be adversely affected if, in particular, the merged entity were likely to use its buyer power vis-à-vis its suppliers to foreclose its rivals[78].

---

[75] Commission Decision 2001/98/EC in Case IV/M.1439 – Telia/Telenor, OJ L 40, 9.2.2001, p. 1, points 330-331, and Case IV/M.1681 – Akzo Nobel/Hoechst Roussel Vet, point 64.

[76] Case IV/M.1630 – Air Liquide/BOC, point 219; Commission Decision 2002/164/EC in Case COMP/M.1853 – EDF/EnBW, OJ L 59, 28.2.2002, p. 1, points 54-64.

[77] See Commission Decision 1999/674/EC in Case M.1221 – Rewe/Meinl, OJ L 274, 23.10.1999, p. 1, points 71-74.

[78] Case T-22/97, Kesko v Commission, [1999] ECR II-3775, paragraph 157; Commission Decision 2002/156/EC in Case M.877 – Boeing/ McDonnell Douglas, OJ L 336, 8.12.1997, p. 16, points 105-108.

62. On the other hand, increased buyer power may be beneficial for competition. If increased buyer power lowers input costs without restricting downstream competition or total output, then a proportion of these cost reductions are likely to be passed onto consumers in the form of lower prices.

63. In order to assess whether a merger would significantly impede effective competition by creating or strengthening buyer power, an analysis of the competitive conditions in upstream markets and an evaluation of the possible positive and negative effects described above are therefore required.

V.   Countervailing buyer power

64. The competitive pressure on a supplier is not only exercised by competitors but can also come from its customers. Even firms with very high market shares may not be in a position, post-merger, to significantly impede effective competition, in particular by acting to an appreciable extent independently of their customers, if the latter possess countervailing buyer power[79]. Countervailing buyer power in this context should be understood as the bargaining strength that the buyer has vis-à-vis the seller in commercial negotiations due to its size, its commercial significance to the seller and its ability to switch to alternative suppliers.

65. The Commission considers, when relevant, to what extent customers will be in a position to counter the increase in market power that a merger would otherwise be likely to create. One source of countervailing buyer power would be if a customer could credibly threaten to resort, within a reasonable timeframe, to alternative sources of supply should the supplier decide to increase prices[80] or to otherwise deteriorate quality or the conditions of delivery. This would be the case if the buyer could immediately switch to other

---

[79]   See, e.g. Case IV/M.1882 — Pirelli/BICC, points 73-80.
[80]   See, e.g. Case IV/M.1245 — Valeo/ITT Industries, point 26.

suppliers[81], credibly threaten to vertically integrate into the upstream market or to sponsor upstream expansion or entry[82] for instance by persuading a potential entrant to enter by committing to placing large orders with this company. It is more likely that large and sophisticated customers will possess this kind of countervailing buyer power than smaller firms in a fragmented industry[83]. A buyer may also exercise countervailing buying power[84] by refusing to buy other products produced by the supplier or, particularly in the case of durable goods, delaying purchases.

66. In some cases, it may be important to pay particular attention to the incentives of buyers to utilise their buyer power. For example, a downstream firm may not wish to make an investment in sponsoring new entry if the benefits of such entry in terms of lower input costs could also be reaped by its competitors.

67. Countervailing buyer power cannot be found to sufficiently offset potential adverse effects of a merger if it only ensures that a particular segment of customers[85], with particular bargaining strength, is shielded from significantly higher prices or deteriorated condi-

---

[81] Even a small number of customers may not have sufficient buyer power if they are to a large extent 'locked in' because of high switching costs (see Case COMP/M.2187 − CVC/Lenzing, point 223).

[82] Commission Decision 1999/641/EC in Case COMP/M.1225 − Enso/Stora, OJ L 254, 29.9.1999, p. 9, points 89-91.

[83] It may also be appropriate to compare the concentration existing on the customer side with the concentration on the supply side (Case COMP/JV 55 − Hutchison/RCPM/ECT, point 119, and Commission Decision 1999/641/EC in Case COMP/M.1225 − Enso/Stora, OJ L 254, 29.9.1999, p. 9, point 97).

[84] Case COMP/JV 55 − Hutchison/RCPM/ECT, points 129-130.

[85] Commission Decision 2002/156/EC in Case COMP/M.2097 − SCA/Metsä Tissue, OJ L 57, 27.2.2002, point 88. Price discrimination between different categories of customers may be relevant in some cases in the context of market definition (See the Commission's notice on the definition of the relevant market, cited above, at paragraph 43).

tions after the merger[86]. Furthermore, it is not sufficient that buyer power exists prior to the merger, it must also exist and remain effective following the merger. This is because a merger of two suppliers may reduce buyer power if it thereby removes a credible alternative.

VI. Entry

68. When entering a market is sufficiently easy, a merger is unlikely to pose any significant anti-competitive risk. Therefore, entry analysis constitutes an important element of the overall competitive assessment. For entry to be considered a sufficient competitive constraint on the merging parties, it must be shown to be likely, timely and sufficient to deter or defeat any potential anti-competitive effects of the merger.

Likelihood of entry

69. The Commission examines whether entry is likely or whether potential entry is likely to constrain the behaviour of incumbents post-merger. For entry to be likely, it must be sufficiently profitable taking into account the price effects of injecting additional output into the market and the potential responses of the incumbents. Entry is thus less likely if it would only be economically viable on a large scale, thereby resulting in significantly depressed price levels. And entry is likely to be more difficult if the incumbents are able to protect their market shares by offering long-term contracts or giving targeted pre-emptive price reductions to those customers that the entrant is trying to acquire. Furthermore, high risk and costs of failed entry may make entry less likely. The costs of failed entry will be higher, the higher is the level of sunk cost associated with entry[87].

---

[86] Accordingly, the Commission may assess whether the various purchasers will hold countervailing buyer power, see, e.g. Commission Decision 1999/641/EC in Case COMP/M.1225 − Enso/Stora, OJ L 254, 29.9.1999, p. 9, points 84-97.
[87] Commission Decision 97/610/EC in Case IV/M.774 − Saint-Gobain/Wacker-Chemie/NOM, OJ L 247, 10.9.1997, p. 1, point 184.

70. Potential entrants may encounter barriers to entry which determine entry risks and costs and thus have an impact on the profitability of entry. Barriers to entry are specific features of the market, which give incumbent firms advantages over potential competitors. When entry barriers are low, the merging parties are more likely to be constrained by entry. Conversely, when entry barriers are high, price increases by the merging firms would not be significantly constrained by entry. Historical examples of entry and exit in the industry may provide useful information about the size of entry barriers.

71. Barriers to entry can take various forms:

(a) Legal advantages encompass situations where regulatory barriers limit the number of market participants by, for example, restricting the number of licences[88]. They also cover tariff and non-tariff trade barriers[89].

(b) The incumbents may also enjoy technical advantages, such as preferential access to essential facilities, natural resources[90], innovation and R & D[91], or intellectual property rights[92], which make it difficult for any firm to compete successfully. For instance, in certain industries, it might be difficult to obtain essential input materials, or patents might protect products or processes. Other factors such as

---

[88] Case IV/M.1430 − Vodafone/Airtouch, point 27; Case IV/M.2016 − France Télécom/Orange, point 33.
[89] Commission Decision 2002/174/EC in Case COMP/M.1693 − Alcoa/Reynolds, OJ L 58, 28.2.2002, point 87.
[90] Commission Decision 95/335/EC in Case IV/M.754 − Anglo American Corp./Lonrho, OJ L 149, 20.5.1998, p. 21, points 118-119.
[91] Commission Decision 97/610/EC in Case IV/M.774 − Saint-Gobain/Wacker-Chemie/NOM, OJ L 247, 10.9.1997, p. 1, points 184-187.
[92] Commission Decision 94/811/EC in Case IV/M.269 − Shell/Montecatini, OJ L 332, 22.12.1994, p. 48, point 32.5.2.2004 EN Official Journal of the European Union C 31/17

economies of scale and scope, distribution and sales networks[93], access to important technologies, may also constitute barriers to entry.

(c) Furthermore, barriers to entry may also exist because of the established position of the incumbent firms on the market. In particular, it may be difficult to enter a particular industry because experience or reputation is necessary to compete effectively, both of which may be difficult to obtain as an entrant. Factors such as consumer loyalty to a particular brand[94], the closeness of relationships between suppliers and customers, the importance of promotion or advertising, or other advantages relating to reputation[95] will be taken into account in this context. Barriers to entry also encompass situations where the incumbents have already committed to building large excess capacity[96], or where the costs faced by customers in switching to a new supplier may inhibit entry.

72. The expected evolution of the market should be taken into account when assessing whether or not entry would be profitable. Entry is more likely to be profitable in a market that is expected to experience high growth in the future[97] than in a market that is mature or expected to decline[98]. Scale economies or network effects may make entry unprofitable unless the entrant can obtain a sufficiently large market share[99].

---

[93] Commission Decision 98/327/EC in Case IV/M.833 – The Coca-Cola Company/Carlsberg A/S, OJ L 145, 15.5.1998, p. 41, point 74.

[94] Commission Decision 98/327/EC in Case IV/M.833 – The Coca-Cola Company/Carlsberg A/S, OJ L 145, 15.5.1998, p. 41, points 72-73.

[95] Commission Decision 2002/156/EC in Case COMP/M.2097 – SCA/Metsä Tissue, OJ L 57, 27.2.2002, p. 1, points 83-84.

[96] Commission Decision 2001/432/EC in Case IV/M.1813 – Industri Kapital Nordkem/Dyno, OJ L 154, 9.6.2001, p. 41, point 100.

[97] See, e.g. Commission Decision 98/475/EC in Case IV/M.986 – Agfa-Gevaert/Dupont, OJ L 211, 29.7.1998, p. 22, points 84-85.

[98] Case T-102/96, Gencor v Commission, [1999] ECR II-753, paragraph 237.

[99] See, e.g. Commission Decision 2000/718/EC in Case IV/M.1578 – Sanitec/Sphinx, OJ L 294, 22.11.2000, p. 1, point 114.

73. Entry is particularly likely if suppliers in other markets already possess production facilities that could be used to enter the market in question, thus reducing the sunk costs of entry. The smaller the difference in profitability between entry and non-entry prior to the merger, the more likely such a reallocation of production facilities.

Timeliness

74. The Commission examines whether entry would be sufficiently swift and sustained to deter or defeat the exercise of market power. What constitutes an appropriate time period depends on the characteristics and dynamics of the market, as well as on the specific capabilities of potential entrants[100]. However, entry is normally only considered timely if it occurs within two years.

Sufficiency

75. Entry must be of sufficient scope and magnitude to deter or defeat the anti-competitive effects of the merger[101]. Small-scale entry, for instance into some market 'niche', may not be considered sufficient.

VII. Efficiencies

76. Corporate reorganisations in the form of mergers may be in line with the requirements of dynamic competition and are capable of increasing the competitiveness of industry, thereby improving the conditions of growth and raising the standard of living in the Community[102]. It is possible that efficiencies brought about by a merger counteract the effects on competition and in particular the potential harm to consumers that it might otherwise have[103]. In or-

---

[100] See, e.g. Commission Decision 2002/174/EC in Case COMP/M.1693 — Alcoa/Reynolds, L 58, 28.2.2002, points 31-32, 38.
[101] Commission Decision 91/535/EEC in Case IV/M.68 — Tetra Pak/Alfa Laval, OJ L 290, 22.10.1991, p. 35, point 3.4.
[102] See Recital 4 of the Merger Regulation.
[103] See Recital 29 of the Merger Regulation.

der to assess whether a merger would significantly impede effective competition, in particular through the creation or the strengthening of a dominant position, within the meaning of Article 2(2) and (3) of the Merger Regulation, the Commission performs an overall competitive appraisal of the merger. In making this appraisal, the Commission takes into account the factors mentioned in Article 2(1), including the development of technical and economic progress provided that it is to the consumers' advantage and does not form an obstacle to competition.[104]

77. The Commission considers any substantiated efficiency claim in the overall assessment of the merger. It may decide that, as a consequence of the efficiencies that the merger brings about, there are no grounds for declaring the merger incompatible with the common market pursuant to Article 2(3) of the Merger Regulation. This will be the case when the Commission is in a position to conclude on the basis of sufficient evidence that the efficiencies generated by the merger are likely to enhance the ability and incentive of the merged entity to act pro-competitively for the benefit of consumers, thereby counteracting the adverse effects on competition which the merger might otherwise have.

78. For the Commission to take account of efficiency claims in its assessment of the merger and be in a position to reach the conclusion that as a consequence of efficiencies, there are no grounds for declaring the merger to be incompatible with the common market, the efficiencies have to benefit consumers, be merger-specific and be verifiable. These conditions are cumulative.

Benefit to consumers

79. The relevant benchmark in assessing efficiency claims is that consumers[105] will not be worse off as a result of the merger. For that

---

[104] Cf. Article 2(1)(b) of the Merger Regulation.
[105] Pursuant to Article 2(1)(b), the concept of 'consumers' encompasses intermediate and ultimate consumers, i.e. users of the products covered by the merger. In other

purpose, efficiencies should be substantial and timely, and should, in principle, benefit consumers in those relevant markets where it is otherwise likely that competition concerns would occur.

80. Mergers may bring about various types of efficiency gains that can lead to lower prices or other benefits to consumers. For example, cost savings in production or distribution may give the merged entity the ability and incentive to charge lower prices following the merger. In line with the need to ascertain whether efficiencies will lead to a net benefit to consumers, cost efficiencies that lead to reductions in variable or marginal costs[106] are more likely to be relevant to the assessment of efficiencies than reductions in fixed costs; the former are, in principle, more likely to result in lower prices for consumers [107]. Cost reductions, which merely result from anti-competitive reductions in output, cannot be considered as efficiencies benefiting consumers.

81. Consumers may also benefit from new or improved products or services, for instance resulting from efficiency gains in the sphere of R & D and innovation. A joint venture company set up in order to develop a new product may bring about the type of efficiencies that the Commission can take into account.

82. In the context of coordinated effects, efficiencies may increase the merged entity's incentive to increase production and reduce prices, and thereby reduce its incentive to coordinate its market behaviour with other firms in the market. Efficiencies may therefore lead to a lower risk of coordinated effects in the relevant market.

---

words, consumers within the meaning of this provision include the customers, potential and/or actual, of the parties to the merger.

[106] Variable costs should be viewed as those costs that vary with the level of production or sales over the relevant time period. Marginal costs are those costs associated with expanding production or sales at the margin.

[107] Generally, fixed cost savings are not given such weight as the relationship between fixed costs and consumer prices is normally less direct, at least in the short run.

83. In general, the later the efficiencies are expected to materialise in the future, the less weight the Commission can assign to them. This implies that, in order to be considered as a counteracting factor, the efficiencies must be timely.

84. The incentive on the part of the merged entity to pass efficiency gains on to consumers is often related to the existence of competitive pressure from the remaining firms in the market and from potential entry. The greater the possible negative effects on competition, the more the Commission has to be sure that the claimed efficiencies are substantial, likely to be realised, and to be passed on, to a sufficient degree, to the consumer. It is highly unlikely that a merger leading to a market position approaching that of a monopoly, or leading to a similar level of market power, can be declared compatible with the common market on the ground that efficiency gains would be sufficient to counteract its potential anti-competitive effects.

Merger specificity

85. Efficiencies are relevant to the competitive assessment when they are a direct consequence of the notified merger and cannot be achieved to a similar extent by less anticompetitive alternatives. In these circumstances, the efficiencies are deemed to be caused by the merger and thus, merger-specific[108]. It is for the merging parties to provide in due time all the relevant information necessary to demonstrate that there are no less anticompetitive, realistic and attainable alternatives of a non-concentrative nature (e.g. a licensing agreement, or a cooperative joint venture) or of a concentrative nature (e.g. a concentrative joint venture, or a differently structured merger) than the notified merger which preserve the claimed efficiencies. The Commission only considers alternatives that are reasonably practical in the business situation faced by the merging par-

---

[108] In line with the general principle set out in paragraph 9 of this notice.

ties having regard to established business practices in the industry concerned.

Verifiability

86. Efficiencies have to be verifiable such that the Commission can be reasonably certain that the efficiencies are likely to materialise, and be substantial enough to counteract a merger's potential harm to consumers. The more precise and convincing the efficiency claims are, the better the Commission can evaluate the claims. Where reasonably possible, efficiencies and the resulting benefit to consumers should therefore be quantified. When the necessary data are not available to allow for a precise quantitative analysis, it must be possible to foresee a clearly identifiable positive impact on consumers, not a marginal one. In general, the longer the start of the efficiencies is projected into the future, the less probability the Commission may be able to assign to the efficiencies actually being brought about.

87. Most of the information, allowing the Commission to assess whether the merger will bring about the sort of efficiencies that would enable it to clear a merger, is solely in the possession of the merging parties. It is, therefore, incumbent upon the notifying parties to provide in due time all the relevant information necessary to demonstrate that the claimed efficiencies are merger-specific and likely to be realised. Similarly, it is for the notifying parties to show to what extent the efficiencies are likely to counteract any adverse effects on competition that might otherwise result from the merger, and therefore benefit consumers.

88. Evidence relevant to the assessment of efficiency claims includes, in particular, internal documents that were used by the management to decide on the merger, statements from the management to the owners and financial markets about the expected efficiencies, historical examples of efficiencies and consumer benefit, and pre-merger external experts' studies on the type and size of efficiency gains, and on the extent to which consumers are likely to benefit.

VIII. Failing firm

89. The Commission may decide that an otherwise problematic merger is nevertheless compatible with the common market if one of the merging parties is a failing firm. The basic requirement is that the deterioration of the competitive structure that follows the merger cannot be said to be caused by the merger[109]. This will arise where the competitive structure of the market would deteriorate to at least the same extent in the absence of the merger[110].

90. The Commission considers the following three criteria to be especially relevant for the application of a 'failing firm defence'. First, the allegedly failing firm would in the near future be forced out of the market because of financial difficulties if not taken over by another undertaking. Second, there is no less anti-competitive alternative purchase than the notified merger. Third, in the absence of a merger, the assets of the failing firm would inevitably exit the market[111].

91. It is for the notifying parties to provide in due time all the relevant information necessary to demonstrate that the deterioration of the competitive structure that follows the merger is not caused by the merger.

---

[109] Joined Cases C-68/94 and C-30/95, Kali and Salz, paragraph 110.

[110] Joined Cases C-68/94 and C-30/95, Kali and Salz, paragraph 114. See also Commission Decision 2002/365/EC in Case COMP/M.2314 — BASF/Pantochim/Eurodiol, OJ L 132, 17.5.2002, p. 45, points 157-160. This requirement is linked to the general principle set out in paragraph 9 of this notice.

[111] The inevitability of the assets of the failing firm leaving the market in question may, in particular in a case of merger to monopoly, underlie a finding that the market share of the failing firm would in any event accrue to the other merging party. See Joined Cases C-68/94 and C-30/95, Kali and Salz, paragraphs 115-116.

Veröffentlichungen des Instituts für deutsches und europäisches Wirtschafts-, Wettbewerbs- und Regulierungsrecht der Freien Universität Berlin

Herausgegeben von Franz Jürgen Säcker

Band 1   Franz Jürgen Säcker (Hrsg.): Deutsch-russisches Energie- und Bergrecht im Vergleich. Ergebnisse einer Arbeitstagung vom 31. März / 1. April 2006. 2007.

Band 2   Franz Jürgen Säcker / Walther Busse von Colbe (Hrsg.): Wettbewerbsfördernde Anreizregulierung. Zum Anreizregulierungsbericht der Bundesnetzagentur vom 30. Juni 2006. 2007.

Band 3   Dirk Zschenderlein: Die Gleichbehandlung der Aktionäre bei der Auskunftserteilung in der Aktiengesellschaft. Zum Problem der Zulässigkeit der Weitergabe von Informationen an einzelne Aktionäre und Dritte. 2007.

Band 4   Simone Kirchhain: Die Anwendung der Vertikal-GVO auf innerstaatliche Wettbewerbsbeschränkungen nach der 7. GWB-Novelle. 2007.

Band 5   Franz Jürgen Säcker: Der Independent System Operator. Ein neues institutionelles Design für Netzbetreiber? 2007.

Band 6   Stefanie Otto: Allgemeininteressen im neuen UWG. § 1 S. 2 UWG und die wettbewerbsfunktionale Auslegung. 2007.

Band 7   Jochen Eichler: Vertragliche Dritthaftung. Eine Auseinandersetzung mit der Frage der Dritthaftung von sogenannten Experten und anderen Auskunftspersonen im Rahmen des § 311 Abs. 3 BGB. 2007.

Band 8   Markela Stamati: Die Anforderungen der operationellen Entflechtung nach den Beschleunigungsrichtlinien der Europäischen Kommission. Umsetzung in Deutschland und Griechenland. 2008.

Band 9   Franz Jürgen Säcker: The Concept of the Relevant Product Market. Between Demand-Side Substitutability and Supply-Side - Substitutability in Competition Law. 2008.

www.peterlang.de